Skating to Sochi

Beverley Smith

Photo Credits

Gerard Chataigneau: Cover, 15, 17, 18, 23, 25, 28, 31, 33, 34, 40, 55, 61, 66, 69, 73, 74, 77, 80, 87, 89, 92, 98, 100, 105, 108, 111, 117, 123, 125, 131, 134, 136, 140, 143, 145, 147, 149, 150, 153, 155, 158, 163, 165, 167, 170, 172

Stephan Potopnyk: 21, 36, 38, 43, 45, 48, 50, 52, 56, 58, 63, 83, 95, 102, 107, 114, 119, 120, 127, 128

ISBN: 978-1-304-51700-5

Cover and interior design: Hartley Millson

Acknowledgments

First and foremost, this book is a tribute to figure skating photographer Gerard Chataigneau, who died suddenly on Nov. 12, 2012. His photos grace this book, which is dedicated to the man whose exquisite art and humble, kind nature should not be forgotten. He intended to take the road to Sochi, so this book will be his final reach to a dream.

Doreen Chataigneau granted the time and generosity so that her husband's photos could appear in this book. Without her help, this book would not exist. And because of her husband, this book had to exist.

Stephan Potopnyk stepped up too, providing photos that Chataigneau didn't have the opportunity to shoot. Potopnyk? Another gentleman of the figure skating world.

Gay Abbate, whose support for this undertaking (and for me) never wavered, and whose editing skills were totally appreciated.

All of the folks at Lulu and their representatives, who turned out a professional product for my first self-publishing endeavour. A special thanks to David Watkins in Hamilton.

Steve Tustin, who always had my back and gave me the confidence to do the job I knew I could do. It means a lot.

My parents, Charles and Edith Smith and brother Michael, who are always there for me, no matter what.

Robbie King Jr., who encouraged me never to give up on this project.

Barb Strain and Steve Milton, who helped along the way.

Skate Canada, for providing their assistance in making this plan work, too.

Jean MacLellan and Rahy's Attorney, whose support is gratefully appreciated.

David and Karen Simmonds, the whiz kids who helped me with photo software.

Fred Dixon, the cheerful and intrepid searcher of hard drives.

All of the skaters and coaches and officials, everywhere, who opened their hearts to interviews.

Contents

Introduction

Russia had never staged a winter Olympics, not until Sochi 2014. It will be a Winter Olympics like no other, partly because it will be held in a seaside resort that is the unofficial summer capital of the country. Greater Sochi is the longest city in Europe, winding for 145 kilometres (90 miles) around the Black Sea, unusual with its extravagant Stalinist architecture, and emboldened with millions of dollars of construction to bring it up to Olympic snuff. It is part of Russian president Vladimir Putin's pitch to the world that the former gloomy days of the Soviet Union are over and that the new Russia is now an international economic force. With its athletes, Russia will put a human face on it, but it needs a storybook ending, not the one it got at the 2010 Vancouver Olympics, where its figure skaters, once the dominant power in the sport, earned no gold medals at all for the first time since 1960.

The Russians are trying to turn their fortunes around in only four years, energetically pouring money into winter sport to erase those nagging memories from Vancouver. "Four years isn't much, but at the same time, it's not few," said Russian pair coach Nina Mozer. "I think we can turn things around. We have already had good results. This new funding will help not only the leading athletes but the young athletes coming up."

Russia hopes to make new memories by the salty sea at a Games that will be a litmus test for the entire sport, what with its new team event, its judging system that is not quite perfect yet, and with the ever increasing athleticism and risk in the sport. While Evan Lysacek of the United States won the men's event at the Vancouver Olympics four years ago with no quadruple jump in his repertoire, it will not be enough in Sochi; call it the Quad Games right now. New rules adopted since the Vancouver Games have made this possible. It is now "higher, faster, stronger" again in figure skating. Can Russian skaters run fast enough to catch up?

So how could Russian skating fall so far so fast? "Vancouver was probably our worst results for winter sports," said 1984 Olympic pair champion Oleg Vasiliev, who coached Russians Tatiana Totmianina and Maxim Marinin to a gold pair medal at the 2006 Turin Olympics. Totmianina and Marinin marked the end of an era of state-funded Soviet sport. Turin was its last flash of Olympic glory. Stars like Evgeny Plushenko, Olympic ice dancing champions Tatiana Navka and Roman Kostomarov and women's star Irina Slutskaya – all medalists in Turin – started their lessons and trained through the old Soviet sports system that allowed them top coaches, financing and everything they needed to succeed.

Then, during the early 1990s, the Soviet Union collapsed, and with it, that finely tuned sport system. The Russian athletes who contested Vancouver grew up in an economically depressed time. "It was terrible," Vasiliev said. "There was no money. People were wondering how to buy bread. Resources were limited. The shelves of the stores were empty. It was a terrible time at the beginning of the 1990s. And that was exactly the time that skaters started for the 2010 Olympics – 17 to 18 years before the Games."

Vasiliev's pair team of Maria Mukhortova and Maxim Trankov who competed at the Vancouver Games fumbled with the changes in their country. Trankov was a throwback from the past who hung on for the love of it, living with little, sleeping on benches, begging for food. This team, like many if your name wasn't Evgeny Plushenko, didn't get the financing they needed. Mukhortova had left a small town in Russia at the age of 13 to train, but she came from a poor family that could not afford the ice costs – think 12,000 rubles ($300 CAD) an hour, when skaters need perhaps six hours every day. Mukhortova and Trankov had little money to train, let alone buy food. Vasiliev gave Mukhortova money, which also helped her mother and grandmother to survive. They had lived in a single room, no larger than 16 square metres. It's not a recipe for success.

While Mukhortova and Trankov scrimped and starved to stay in the sport, many of Russia's competitive skaters just couldn't stick around. Mozer, coach of current world pair champions Tatiana Volosozhar and Maxim Trankov, said Russia lost many skaters to shows: Holiday on Ice, Disney On Ice, even cruise ships because there was no financial support to continue on the competitive track. Also she said Russian skating suffered from the long, upper-crust careers of skaters such as Plushenko, unbeatable for years whenever he set foot onto the ice. Skaters like Andrei Griazev and Sergei Dobrin found it psychologically hard, she said. They lost their joy of competing and when they did, they were afraid of making errors, trying to live up to legends. In his early days, Griazev, born in 1985, was compared to 1998 Olympic champion Ilia Kulik, but he was never able to realize the promise, felled partly by injury. He survived by teaching young skaters and relying on the largesse of his coaches Taitiana Tarasova and Alexei Yagudin – indeed he lived with Tarasova while training in Connecticut – and sometimes by skating in skating tours organized by retired Russian ice dancer Ilia Averbukh. But Griazev retired in 2009, before he ever got to Vancouver. "None of the young ones were able to break through for 10 years," Mozer said. "That's why many of the young ones gave up and left for the shows. So in 2006 we suddenly found out that we didn't have any young ones." For about 10 years, Russia suffered from a dearth of young skaters signing up at costly figure skating clubs.

The skaters weren't the only ones affected: Coaches were starving too. Russia lost more than 400 coaches who found that they could earn as much in one day in North America as it would take in a year to earn in Russia. Mozer left, too, and worked in Chicago for several years, but returned to Russia in 2002, partly because she found the American way of doing things "was not very interesting for me." She was troubled by the system: athletes might be in the midst of learning something important, but the lesson would abruptly end. After all, they had paid for only an hour, for example. "Everything was so limited," she said. "Money is not the most important thing for me. I want to work to achieve a result. In the United States, if you have enough money, you can continue to work. If you don't have enough money, you can't. For us, I have observed mostly those athletes who don't have so much money. They are the ones that are successful."

For two Olympics, Russians were also held back when their skating coaches resisted the new scoring system that came into play after the judging scandals of the 2002 Salt Lake City Olympics. In the old 6.0 system, judges would submit two numbers, one for technical merit, the other for artistic impression or presentation, allowing enormous room for subjective opinion, sometimes routed by deal-making. But the new system was much more diligent about examining every detail in a skater's routine and giving it a score, right down to the turns and footwork between elements. It is also exceedingly complex: jumps are assigned points depending on how difficult they are and other elements, like spins, have levels of difficulty (level one to level four, with level four being the toughest, worth more points); skaters can pick up bonuses if they perform jumps and elements extremely well, but they can lose points if they don't; skaters get a 10 per cent bonus for doing jumps in the second half of their programs, when their lungs are bursting; the old artistic or presentation marks (now called program components) are broken down into five categories (skating skills, transition or linking elements, performance and execution, choreography and composition and interpretation), marked out of 10, and added onto the technical mark to produce a single number, a score.

Strategy is everything. Should you attempt an easier element, knowing you can do it really well and get bonus marks? Or risk a difficult element that is worth more, but do it badly and lose points for grade of execution? "Russia was a little late catching up with the new system," Mozer admitted. "The other countries went forward and we were still working as if the old system was in place. We didn't take the new system too seriously. Then we realized that the new system is going to be there forever and we started to catch up. Now we have some very strong young athletes that have grown up with the new system."

Also for the first time many Russian coaches – even seventysomething Alexei Mishin – are turning to North American choreographers who do understand the system. But alas, some of the injury problems swamping young Russian athletes stem from their struggle to catch up to the new system. "They were lacking the basic skills, and because they were trying to do things they couldn't really do, they got injured," Mozer said.

Still, for all of its changes, or perhaps as a result of it, Russia faces a strange paradox in figure skating popularity. A figure skating ticket has never been more highly valued in Russia these days, but it's not for the competitive events. Russians are flocking to skating tours and shows that feature celebrities. Ilia Averbukh, a former Olympic silver medalist, has no trouble selling out tours in 54 cities, and attracting large pools of sponsors to plug cosmetics, sportswear and drinks. Indeed, Averbukh's shows are a drop in the bucket. Agent Ari Zakarian notes that currently in Russia, there are 400 to 500 shows a year, while in the United States, tours and shows are shrinking to a shadow of what they had been during the 1990s. (In 2000, the popular Stars On Ice stopped at 65 cities in the United States, but last year, only six and the Champions on Ice tour disappeared years ago.) Sponsors aren't flocking to Russian skating competitions, however. Still, the recent pre-Olympic support from Russian authorities – hiring teams that include medical and other specialties to bring out the best in skaters – has made it possible for the next generation to regain a foothold in the sport. Now there are promising athletes like Maxim Kovtun and a host of young female skaters rushing onto the world scene. Will they be ready in time for Sochi? Will Kovtun still be overshadowed by Plushenko, dragging his weary body to the plate, attempting to make his fourth Olympics?

Russia's best chance for a gold medal at the Sochi Olympics will come from irrepressible pair skaters Volosozhar and Trankov, who won their first world title at the 2013 championships by a landslide – by 20 points. Russia's first Olympic medal in figure skating came from Soviet pair team Ludmila Belousova and Oleg Protopopov, so it's only fitting that 50 years later, Russia can field a pair that can send shivers down the spines of all competitors. But Russia will have to hope that its skaters from the other disciplines can join forces to win a gold medal in a figure skating team event that will be offered for the first time at the Sochi Games. The model on which the team event is based is the World Team Trophy in Japan that is held a couple of weeks after the world championships.

Although the Japanese federations and Japanese television networks have sunk enormous finances into the World Team Trophy, paying all the costs of skaters, coaches, federation members, judges and first-class hotel and food accommodation for a larger team event than will appear in Sochi, the World Team Trophy doesn't appear to be taken seriously. It's a festive event, with feather boas around necks, and friendly comraderie among teams. In gymnastics and equestrian sport, the team event offers a prized medal at the Olympics and world championships – and other events, too – but it's been part of the cultures of those sports for many years. "I'm not particularly fond of this event," three-time world champion Patrick Chan told a newspaper afterwards in his candid, no-holds-barred fashion, speaking of the World Team Trophy. (He fell three times in the free skate.) "Nobody's really interested in it. Skating is done after worlds…There's no spark, no buzz in the air at the rink." Skaters fear injury when exhausted at the end of a long season. One Russian skater injured a shoulder during the World Team Trophy and will now have to deal with recovery going into an Olympic season, when any setback is troublesome.

And despite what Chan says about the World Team Trophy, the new team event could give Canada an extra medal at the Sochi Olympics. Currently, Canada is favoured for gold. Canada will field the largest team of all countries to the figure skating event in Sochi, with 17 of a possible 18 Olympic berths. Not only that, Canada fielded two skaters who finished among the top six in three of the four disciplines at the 2013 world championships. And it now has a contender, Kaetlyn Osmond, in the women's event in a discipline that has long proved to be a weakness in Canada.

NUMBER OF SKATERS QUALIFIED BY THE TOP FIVE COUNTRIES FOR THE OLYMPIC GAMES					
COUNTRY	WOMEN	MEN	PAIRS	ICE DANCING TEAMS	TOTAL PEOPLE
Canada	2	3	3	3	17
Russia	2	1	3	3	15
United States	3	2	2	3	15
France	1	2	2	2	11
Japan	3	3	0	0	6
There is further qualification at the Nebelhorn Trophy in Germany in Sept. 2013					

Defending Olympic ice dancing champion Scott Moir, who skates with Tessa Virtue, said he's proud of the large Canadian contingent that will go to Sochi. Because of the team event, the entire Canadian team may have to forego the opening ceremonies, usually an issue for only the pair teams, which are first up on the schedule. Although the ice dancing event is a week later, Virtue and Moir will go to the Olympics early – something they say they do anyway. "We are so pumped for that team event," he said. "We also have the opportunity to compete alongside Patrick [Chan], to be honest and we have kind of grown up together in the team event. We have a very solid shot."

Chan's worries aside, the Olympic team event is proving controversial, even though it took ISU president Ottavio Cinquanta eight years to lobby and get a second medal event for figure skaters on the Olympic roster. "It is a new venture," said David Dore, a Canadian who is first vice-president of the International Skating Union. "Will it be perfect? Probably not." The top 10 figure skating countries, determined by a points system based on finishes at world championships and at Grand Prix events during the fall of 2013, will qualify for the Olympic event, with five being eliminated after the short program. After negotiating with the International Olympic Committee (which requires that any skater who competes at the Olympics must have qualified for the Olympics), the ISU reached a compromise that would allow 10 extra spots for skaters who did not qualify for their country's Olympic teams, but were needed to compete in the team event so that a country could be represented in all disciplines. That will help a country that is short of qualifying a skater for one of the four team disciplines. Some substitutions will be allowed during the event. For example, Patrick Chan could skate the short program for Canada, and Kevin Reynolds could skate the long. The team event will start the day before the opening ceremonies and end two days before the pairs individual competition.

But the alteration of the traditional Olympic schedule has many skaters worried. What if they suffer an injury in the team event that will affect their performance later on in the individual event? Will the team event tire out the pair skaters who are first up to compete for individual medals? "We don't know if we're in trouble for the Olympics," Dore said. "Getting this set of medals was not easy. But now that we got it, we don't know how people are going to react. It's an opportunity presenting itself, but people are giving me the downside. All I can say is that I did my best."

Dore does not know if some countries will opt out of the team competition altogether, willing to throw away a medal if they feel strongly about the chances of one of their skaters winning an individual medal. He does not know if powerful countries with a lot of skaters, such as Canada or Russia or the United States, will field only their second-ranked skaters, not their first, to the team event. "My only argument is that I'm giving you a chance to be a double gold medalist, and a double Olympic medalist, according to what I see in the world today, is worth a lot of money," he said.

The team event isn't the end of Dore's concerns about Olympic figure skating events, but he's made it clear there will not be any more rule changes until after the Sochi Games, because he doesn't like "changing the rules in the middle of the game." He admits there is still a problem with the way judges mark program component marks, the ones that track presentation and transitions and performance. "I call Sochi the end of an era," said Dore, because afterwards, there will be an ISU Congress that can bring in rule changes. There has been plenty of criticism that judges don't apply the component marks according to what they see on the ice, either because they are afraid of veering outside an acceptable "corridor" of marks, and therefore being cited for poor judging; or they are using it to prop up a skater to get the result they want. Dore says he's addressing the issue to the ISU's technical committees. He has asked them: "Are we confident that we are where we want to be?"

At the Congress after Sochi, Dore said the ISU will be looking into the component issue, but also the "falling" issue. Currently skaters are penalized a point if they fall. If both skaters on a pair or dance team fall, they lose a total of two points. Is it enough? "Falling is a big discussion," he said. "It's not a five-minute fix. It's not going to be a band-aid solution." If you penalize falls too heavily, will you also discourage risk? Will spectators be turned off by the sight of constant falls?

And what is more risky than a quadruple jump? The quad, in slumber mode during the Vancouver Olympics, awakened with a vengeance after the ISU made two rule changes that not only raised the value of the jump but also lowered the penalties for failing to complete the four rotations. While the quadruple toe loop was worth 9.80 points during Vancouver Olympic season, it's worth 10.30 points now (not counting bonus points for how well it's executed.) However, the major incentive for skaters to begin ramping up their quad practices again, was the reduction of penalties for at least trying it. During the Vancouver Games, if a skater fell on a quad – as long as he got the full four rotations in – he'd still get about five or six points. If he didn't fall, but underrotated the quad, the punishment was more severe; He could end up with only one point for his trouble. But beginning in 2010-2011, the ISU established a two-tier system for underrotating jumps, depending on how serious the underrotation was. The penalty is still severe if the jump just goes bad and a skater falls short by half a rotation or more. But if the underroration is slight, by less than one-quarter of a rotation – something that is often invisible to the naked eye of even an experienced observer – the skater still gets to keep about 70 per cent of the points, a reward for a valiant effort.

Patricia Chafe, a Skate Canada consultant whose company, Jump Beyond, creates strategies for skaters to make best use of the judging system, said the quick resurgence of the quad jump surprised her. "I was shocked at how fast the transition happened [after the rule change]," she said. Chan introduced his quads to his repertoire at the beginning of that 2010-2011 season. It propelled him immediately to the top and he hasn't lost a world championship since. Chafe warned that the increase in risk would initially be accompanied by a rise in falls, as skaters worked to master the difficult jump. The values of all the jumps changed that year.

The male skaters have been raising the bar on quads every year, to the point that during the pre-Olympic season, two skaters won championship gold medals with three quads in their long program: Kevin Reynolds of Canada at the Four Continents championship in Osaka, Japan, and Javier Fernandez of Spain at the European championships in Zagreb, Croatia. Fernandez's coach, Brian Orser, hinted that Fernandez is thinking of doing four quads in his free program, something that has never been done before. "Good for him," Orser said. "He might surprise himself.…It might be necessary for [Olympic] year, but it's doable. I'm always for raising the bar. Even if you are a front runner, you need to keep raising the bar. Because the second you don't, that's when people come up and BOOM, and the ones you least expect are there."

Chan has been on his own at the top for the past couple of years, but now his competitors want to beat him at his own game: skating choreography, Orser said. "Now he's not the only one doing quads. And now you have some of the skaters who have the whole package, which is the choreography and the skating skills, the intricate steps." It's never been so difficult to win an Olympic gold medal.

But try they will, aiming for a brass ring that comes along every four years. The skaters in the following pages are the world's best, the ones who will make Sochi memorable, the ones with their hearts and minds set on Olympic glory. Some have been training for a decade or more for this moment. They are a varied group, all with different stories and paths and cultures, all meeting on the same ice with a common purpose. The Olympic atmosphere affects people differently: It raises some to dizzying heights of accomplishment, but defeats others. The line between success and utter defeat will be small, a momentary lapse, a twizzle gone wrong in a fleeting second, a skater finding an uncommon zone. Evan Lysacek won his Olympic gold medal by 1.31 points. At an Olympic Games, there are always surprises.

Women

Mao **Asada**

Japan

Born: Sept. 25, 1990

Coaches: Nobuo and Kumiko Sato

Best Results: silver medal at 2010 Olympics, two-time world champion

*I*F THE MEASURE OF A PERSON CAN BE TAKEN AT THE DARKEST OF TIMES, THEN PUT A STAR BESIDE MAO ASADA'S NAME.

ASADA, LIGHT AND LIVELY ON THE ICE, AND JUST ABOUT TO GATHER HER FORCES, GOT THE NEWS BEFORE THE SHORT PROGRAM AT THE GRAND PRIX FINAL IN QUEBEC CITY IN DECEMBER OF 2011.

Her mother, Kyoto, was in critical condition in hospital with a liver ailment. Asada raced to the airport, but didn't get home to Nagoya in time. Her mother, only 48 years old, died. She'd been a tireless supporter of her skating daughter.

Still, eyes straight ahead, Asada competed at her national championships only weeks later and won it. Then, with grief on her shoulder, she faltered at the world championships, finishing sixth.

The following season, Asada, perhaps recalling the soulful skates of Joannie Rochette, whose mother died while she was at the Vancouver Olympics, had a plan to honour her mother with dirge-like pieces in 2012-13. Her mother, she resolved, should not be forgotten.

Asada arrived at the doorstep of Lori Nichol in May of 2012, to get the design for an exhibition routine only, uncertain of her skating future. "She stayed strong after her mother passed away to try to get through the season," Nichol said. "And I think after worlds, she allowed herself to breathe."

But everything was up in the air about what Asada wanted to do with her career and skating. Her words sounded as if she contemplated retirement. Nichol figured she didn't really mean it: that she just did not want to make any commitments or big decisions. The idea was to take it one day at a time and find joy in skating again. With that in mind, Asada presented Nichol with her ideas for a tribute.

Nichol found the music very dolorous. She told the waif-like Japanese: "You know, I'm a mom. If I passed away, I would like to know that my children are going to go on and live a happy life. Your mother would not want you to be sad on the ice."

So Nichol proposed that they find some music that would bring joy back to her skating. What could be more uplifting than Mary Poppins, even just the sight of her with pert umbrella in hand, soaring over rooftops? "It had her giggling right away," said Nichol, especially when she heard the words and music for the chimney sweep song: "Chim Chiminey, chim chiminey, chim chim cheree. A sweep is as lucky as lucky can be!"

During the process, out from the Nichol vaults sprang the upbeat and joyful "I Got Rhythm."

Asada loved the George Gershwin classic so much, she quickly decided that she wanted to skate her short program to it. And with that, apparently came her decision to continue.

With the Nichol routine and a "Swan Lake" long program choreographed by Russian legend Tatiana Tarasova, Asada regained her power. She swept all her events during the Grand Prix season, including the final. She won the Japanese championships, not an easy task because there are so many talented female singles skaters in Japan. She finished first in both the short and the long programs at the Four Continents championships in Osaka. She finally got back onto the world podium in London, Ont., winning a bronze medal, promising better things to come.

"She was so stoic," Nichol said of Asada's deportment after her mother's death. "I admire her strength and her courage at such a young age. She understood the situation, because that can help you get through something. She understood everything clearly. And she'd been living with it for a long time. She never asked for sympathy or made an excuse. She always stayed strong and true and very honourable about the privacy." She was 21 when her mother died.

During last season, Asada said she rediscovered her joy of skating again. "Every day that I go to the rink, I can't wait to skate again," she said.

Nichol sees Asada as a rare "pure spirit," in an era when it seems good to be bad. What Asada presented – on and off the ice – last year was a wonderful tribute to her mother, that she could raise her daughter to present such dignity, to remain calm amid storms, Nichol said.

She's not a diva, although in Japan she's

worshipped like a rock star, has trails of endorsements, has her own line of kimonos called MaoMao, and halted the release of a biography in 2012 that "was different from what I had in mind," she said.

The rest, everybody knows. Mao was an uncommon prodigy, landing a triple Axel when she was only 13. She became the first to land a triple Axel at the junior world championships, when she was only 14. She became the first to land three triple Axels at the same competition. She landed her first triple, a Salchow, now her least favourite jump, when she was eight or nine.

Everyone knows that she burst upon the scene, coached by Midori Ito's mentor, Machiko Yamada, that she wore Ito hand-me-down costumes in the early days, that she defeated Kim Yu-Na at the 2005 junior world championships in Kitchener, Ont., but she wasn't eligible to the (senior) world championships that followed. Nor was she eligible to the 2006 Olympic Games in Turin, even after having delivered a drubbing to her senior peers at the Grand Prix Final two months before. She did not win her first world title until 2008 in Sweden.

Her triple Axel has been her ultimate weapon, and she has steadfastly insisted on including it in her programs, although many times, an underrotated one has cost her marks and medals. During the 2007-08 season, Asada fell afoul of the increasingly closer scrutiny of elements of a new scoring system, which docked lots of marks for underrotated jumps.

Eventually, after taking lessons from coaches in California and Russia and, for a while nobody at all, Asada eventually sought out Nobuo Sato, a Japanese skating pioneer, who worked to change the technique of her jumps. It has taken years. Asada had just begun to find her footing again when her mother died. Perhaps now she will skate in peace.

Asada will go into Sochi as an Olympic silver medalist from 2010, and a two-time world champion. She says she will hang up her competitive skates after the 2014 Olympic Games. It's been a long hard road, already.

Gracie **Gold**
United States

Born: Aug. 17, 1995

Coaches: Alexander Ouriashev, Oleg Epstein

Best Result: silver medalist at the 2012 world junior championships, 6th at the 2013 world championships

FOR A LONG TIME NOW, PEOPLE HAVE BEEN TELLING GRACIE GOLD TO BRUSH UP ON HER RUSSIAN. OR IN OTHER WORDS, TO COUNT ON COMPETING AT THE SOCHI OLYMPICS. THEY'VE BEEN TELLING HER THIS SINCE SHE WAS A JUNIOR SKATER.

IT'S A BURDEN THAT RESTS, SOMETIMES HEAVILY, ON THE SHOULDERS OF THE petite blond, who looks like a sprite-like latter-day version of Olympic champion Carol Heiss. Since the days of Norwegian Sonja Henie, who glamourized women's skating in the United States with her tours and movies in the 1940s, the women's category in the country has been its Holy Grail. For those who care to indulge, the memories will flow: Olympic champions Tenley Albright, the aforementioned Heiss, Peggy Fleming, Dorothy Hamill, Kristi Yamaguchi, Tara Lipinski, Sarah Hughes, and while we're at it, toss in Linda Fratianne, Rosalynn Sumners, Nancy Kerrigan, Michelle Kwan, Sasha Cohen, Debi Thomas, Janet Lynn, and Mirabel Vinson. Dare we whisper the name of Tonya Harding, who in her own unusual fashion, sparked a deluge of world-wide interest in the sport a couple of decades ago and who always seems good for a headline or two so many years later?

Alas, the United States has been in an uncommon drought, when it comes to females grabbing the gold ring these days. There hasn't been a U.S. female Olympic figure skating champion since Sarah Hughes in 2002. And the most recent U.S. world champion was 16-year-old Kimmie Meissner in 2006. Also, frustratingly enough, beginning in the 2010-11 season, the United States lost its full complement of world championship (and Vancouver Olympic) berths (for only the second time since World War II) dropping from three to two each year since. Only in 2013, did Ashley Wagner and Gracie Gold win all three spots back for 2014 by finishing fifth and sixth at the world championships in London, Ont.

So the mantle fell heavily on Gold's wee shoulders when she began to sparkle precociously as a junior, which is about the time the Americans start looking for their next women's star, though as Gold reminds everyone, she didn't really do anything big until the 2011-2012 season. She failed to qualify for the 2011 U.S. championships. At the time, she wasn't living up to her potential and didn't even imagine she would be there. So indeed, she wasn't.

That all changed the next year when Gold and her coach Alexander Ouriashev, a former

Ukrainian champion, ramped up the technical content of her programs. She got only one Junior Grand Prix event (even though she didn't qualify for it through the usual route – efforts at U.S. championships) and won it. Then she steamrolled her way to victory as the U.S. junior champion, winning with a record score (178.92) and a mighty triple Lutz – triple toe loop combination, something only the best of the big girls do. Her coach told a reporter: "She has some of the best potential as a skater in the United States for the next three years."

Gold had won the junior title at age 16; Kwan had jumped to senior at age 13. Gold's story was to be different, but nonetheless dramatic. She went on to win the silver medal at the world junior figure skating championships in Minsk, sandwiched between two up-and-coming Russian women, Julia Lipnitskaia, who dominated, and Adelina Sotnikova.

Finally during the 2012-13 season, Gold got her first senior Grand Prix assignment – Skate Canada. Really, it was only her third international competition, her first being that little Junior Grand Prix event in Estonia, the second in Minsk. The lights at Skate Canada were brighter and so was the hype.

She finished ninth of 10 in the short program. Asked by a reporter in the mixed zone: "You see an article about how you're the big hope in the United States, and I know that you try not to let that affect you, but does it, a little bit?"

Gold replied: "I think it does with everyone when an article comes out, saying you're the next hope. That's just an extra element of pressure, because you already have pressure from yourself, your expectations, and then to have the public and the US ladies putting the Olympic hope on your shoulders, it does make a bit of difference. I'm just trying to completely ignore it and focus on my skating and why I'm supposed to be here."

She'd hoped to be in the top five at both of her Grand Prix events, but at Skate Canada, she finished seventh overall, losing her hopes of qualifying for the Grand Prix Final.

It was a different story, however, at the Rostelecom Cup in Russia, where she won the short program and the silver medal overall. After that, she admitted that she had been nervous at Skate Canada and had put too much pressure on herself. In Russia, she said she just remembered to take a deep breath and skate the way she does in practice. The medal in Russia gave her a confidence boost.

Again, at U.S. nationals, perhaps under pressure again in front of a home audience, Gold finished only ninth in the short program. But the long program? It was one to remember. Gold unleashed a triple Lutz – triple toe loop combination that was as good as any Olympic gold medalist could land. She skated as if on wings. When she finished, she pumped her fist, winning the free skate and the silver medal to a standing ovation. It was the effort that got her to the world championships in London, where in her debut, she was sixth. "I came to prove myself," she said in London. "The fact that I can land elements well says a lot about me as a competitor."

Gold still has a long road to travel. Her technical elements are formidable. Her jumps are pure and picture perfect. She still needs spit and polish to add value to her presentation (program component mark), but look at Canada's Kaetlyn Osmond. It can be done. And Gold is a perfectionist.

The daughter of Carl, an anaesthiologist and Denise, Gold started skating when she was eight years old, after seeing some skaters spinning on a rink at a friend's birthday party. Her fraternal twin sister, Carly, also competes. They are Golds, after all.

Kim **Yu-Na**
South Korea

Born: Sept 5, 1990

Coaches: Chin Hye-Sook, Rye Jong-Hyun

Best Results: 2010 Olympic champion, two-time world champion

THE AUDIENCE FELL SILENT. JUDGES PEERED THROUGH THEIR SPECS, ANTICIPATING. LITTLE (AND NOT SO LITTLE) GIRLS LEANED FORWARD, READY TO DISPOSE OF THEIR TEDDY BEARS, TO TOSS THEM LOVINGLY ONTO COLD ICE. BY THE END OF THE 2013 WORLD CHAMPIONSHIPS, AFTER 20 MONTHS OF WAITING TO SEE THIS WINSOME SOUTH KOREAN SKATER, THEY ALL FOUND THAT

the glass slipper fit after all. It's not that they had ever doubted it, mind you, but Queen Yu-Na was back.

Hoards watched Kim Yu-Na practice in London, Ont., craning their necks to see how she looked, astonished to see her land very difficult triple-triple jump combinations with such ease, she barely ruffled an eyelash. The practices were workmanlike. Kim did them all, unsmiling, deep within her own thoughts. Her short program performance to "Kiss of the Vampire" was workmanlike, too, with an absence of command, and accordingly, drew no standing ovation. Kim looked astonished at the marks. Her 69.97 points was far short of her world record of 78.50 for the short program that she had earned when she won the 2010 Olympics in Vancouver. Perhaps it wasn't so easy to come back after all.

But Kim puffed herself up for the long program, where she really made her grand entrance back to the skating wars, earning 148.34 points, close to her world record standard of 150.06, set at the 2010 Games. Dressed in pale grey, she came

alive, a mystery unveiling itself, reserved off the ice, but an artist on it. That she had returned at all was surprising. She had intended to retire after the Vancouver Olympics.

It's not so easy being a legend in South Korea, which prizes its stars, especially when they come from a sport that had almost no history in the country. As Kim rose up the skating ranks, her star power became boundless. By the time of the Vancouver Olympics, Kim was drawing an estimated $9-million a year in endorsements, one of the wealthiest female athletes in the world, according to Forbes (No. 7 on the list). She became South Korea's Princess Diana. She could not walk in the streets without attracting crowds or cameramen, hanging on every word, recording every move. "Seeing how every word I speak at interviews gathered so much attention – seeing how the public perception is formed in front of my eyes – made me want to step back from it all just a bit," she said at a press conference in South Korea in 2012, announcing her comeback and her quest for Sochi. It is no wonder that she

escaped to Canada in her run-up to the Vancouver Olympics and then to the United States for one year, before the 2011 world championship in Moscow (where she finished second to Mao Asada.)

But after Moscow, something changed. After five years away from her country, Kim wanted to go home. If going home meant she had to face the music, and the fame she had created, so be it. She was at a stage where she could handle it. "She has grown up," said her long-time choreographer David Wilson. "She started to relax and feel the desire to be home with her people and her friends, to feel in her own element."

She's now more comfortable in her skin, Wilson said. She's grown into her fame. No longer does she get her strength only from skating, he said. She's getting it from within. And she's using it to her country's advantage. After the 2011 world championships, Kim became one of the faces of the PyeongChang bid for the 2018 Winter Olympics. "It was massive," Wilson said. Kim trained just as hard for her speech to the International Olympic Committee in Durban, South Africa, during the summer of 2011 as she had for any skating competition. Three or four months before she was to speak to IOC officials, Kim trained with speech writers and linguistic teachers so that she could deliver her pitch in English. "They trained her like a politician," Wilson said. "And she pulled it off. She clinched the deal." PyeongChang had lost narrowly in two previous bids. This time, the tiny resort town had won. Kim had spent two months travelling the world for the bid.

She contributed in other ways too. A little-known fact about Kim: She's also a singer. She and veteran South Korean singer Lena Park recorded a duet to "Dream of Winter," backed up by soft guitar music, and recorded at a Gangnam studio. Critics said Kim's soft voice complemented Park's strong vocals. All of these were heady accomplishments.

"She went from being a very shy, inward, stone-faced girl seven years ago to now being open, worldly, smart, fun, a fabulous person," Wilson said. "She has a great sense of humour. Now she has a really valuable perspective that not many people have."

While taking a break from skating, Kim went to school to study physical education, the only female in the class. "She liked the experience and worked very hard at it," Wilson said. She also played host to a television show called "Kim Yuna's Kiss and Cry," focused on ten popular Korean entertainers coached to skate by professional skaters. Kim hosted the show with South Korean comedian Shin Dong-Yeop, and also served as a mentor – and judge, too. Kim pulled all the strings.

Kim had found another life. Why return and go through all of the pain of training for another Olympic run? Kim agonized over her future. She was clearly in turmoil. She was at a loss. "I didn't make up my mind easily," she said. She dreaded most the tough practice sessions, to get her skills and particularly her fitness levels back to world class levels. "I was not confident about myself to overcome those painful times again," she said. Her first coach, Rye Jong-Hyun was there to help her, eventually in charge of her fitness and conditioning. Rye was the coach who worked with Kim when she started to skate at age 7.

Kim still continued to work at the Taeneung Training Centre in Seoul, where her early coaches ply their trade. Behind the scenes, Chin Hye-Sook, who had coached Kim between the ages of 10 and 12, gently persuaded Kim to return.

According to a South Korean TV documentary, Chin wrote on a chalkboard usually reserved for music rotations for skaters: "Yuna Kim, let's go for the 2013 world championships." When Kim saw the message, she smilingly erased it, saying: "No way. Impossible thing."

But Chin, who competed at the 1980 Winter Olympics in Lake Placid, N.Y., could see that whenever Kim trained at Taeneung, she still had a will "to do something." As a coach who taught Kim her triple jumps (she in turn got her instruction from a Japanese coach, who used to regularly visit Toronto in the summers with some Japanese students), Chin was always very surprised at Kim's abilities. "Therefore I think it's a waste for her to quit – or retire even at the Sochi Olympics," she told the documentary.

However, Kim had already won Olympic gold in Vancouver. And the effort and all the expectations of a country took a psychological toll on her. She was listless at the 2010 world championships in Turin that followed. She hadn't wanted to go. "She was totally spent," Wilson said. "I'm not so sure her heart was in it."

Kim told a South Korean press conference last year that it was not easy to find motivation to

continue competing. "On the other hand, the love and attention from many in my country and figure skating fans continued to grow," she said. "To be honest, I felt extremely pressured to receive all of your love and attention and it sometimes made me want to escape from it all – for just one day."

She dreaded making mistakes at competitions and failing to fulfill expectations, she said. How could she overcome these pressures? Her year away from competition was "so precious," she said.

However, her answer came from little skaters in her own country. At Taeneung, she found herself trying to help the youngsters, as someone who had forged a path for them. She felt a responsibility to pass on what she knew. But they gave something back to her: motivation. "I was challenged by their hard work on the ice," she said. "It made me think that there must be something I can do as a competitive skater for figure skating in Korea. "

Perhaps, she thought, the worst kind of pressure she felt was the pressure she put on herself. Perhaps, she could lower her expectations of herself and skate for a different reason. She decided to skate, not for medals, but for herself. Besides, if she stopped competing only because of pressures and expectations, she wondered if

she would regret that decision down the road. This new attitude worked out well for her at the 2013 world championships. She won the gold medal by 20.42 points, instantly making herself the favourite for Sochi.

She told the press conference that she would like to make a fresh start, not to be known as Olympic champion, but as a member of the South Korean skating team. She will retire after Sochi, she said. And she'd like to become a member of the IOC Athletes' Commission.

She's become a leader. She donated her $45,000 prize for winning the 2013 world championships to UNICEF to help children with disabilities. After finishing second at the 2011 world championships in Moscow, she also handed over her $27,000 in winnings to the Japanese children affected by the earthquake and tsunami. She's filmed a video message to make an appeal for children suffering from violence in Syria. The Sochi Olympics is only a step along the way. "Perhaps then, my retirement from competitive skating at Sochi would mean yet another start for new dreams and goals in life," she said. By Sochi, she will have been skating for 18 years. For Kim, that's enough. She will be ready to hand off the torch, a force for figure skating in her country and perhaps beyond.

Carolina **Kostner**
Italy

Born: Feb. 8, 1987

Coach: Michael Huth

Best Results: 2012 world champion, five-time European champion, 2011 Grand Prix Final champion

CAROLINA KOSTNER'S VOICE IS LIKE NO OTHER. IT'S POETIC. THERE'S A LYRICAL LILT TO HER WORDS, ALWAYS MEASURED THOUGHTFULLY. PERHAPS IT HAS SOMETHING TO DO WITH HER BIRTHPLACE. ASIDE FROM FOUR WELL-KNOWN LANGUAGES (ITALIAN, GERMAN, FRENCH AND ENGLISH) SHE SPEAKS A MINORITY LANGUAGE, LADIN, THE MOTHER TONGUE

of a cluster of northern Italy provinces, probably spoken by no more than 40,000 people in the world. Indeed, Kostner is unique.

Kostner was born in an Italian mountain valley town, Balzano, the daughter of Patrizia, a former national-level figure skater, and Edwin, who played ice hockey at world championships and Olympics. Her cousin, Isolde Kostner, was a three-time Olympic medalist in alpine skiing. While one side of her family is sports crazy, the other side is steeped in art. Her grandfather was director of the Art Academy in her hometown of Bolzano and Kostner's mother teaches geometric art. Kostner studies art, lives it, breathes it and never more so than on the road to the Sochi Olympics.

Kostner has never had a smooth ride in her figure skating career, but her misfortunes have transformed her into one of the sport's great artists. At the 2013 world championships in London, Ont., Kostner conquered Olympic champion Kim Yu-Na on the program component (or presentation) mark, at least in the short program,

receiving 33.85 points to the South Korean's 33.18 for that segment of the total mark. In the long, Kim found herself, got six perfect 10s, and finished with 73.61 component marks, to Kostner's 70.69. But Kostner's artistic marks were a couple of points higher than the presentation score of exquisite Japanese skater, Mao Asada.

Four years ago, Kostner's career crumbled with injury. She finished only 12th at the 2009 world championships after a long program in which she failed to land a single clean triple jump. And the Olympics have never been kind to her. At the Turin Games close to her hometown, Kostner finished ninth. At the Vancouver Olympics, she was 16th after stumbling and falling on most of her jumps in the free skate. She began to question her future in the sport.

During the 2010-11 season, Kostner suffered a left knee injury and couldn't practice triple Lutzes or triple flips until the end of the Grand Prix season. When the season was over, she took a 2 ½ -month break from skating and escaped surgery by undergoing physiotherapy.

But Lori Nichol, her long-time choreographer, refused to give up on her. Nichol had worked with Kostner since the 2006-07 season and had come to know her soul. "The big change was the year she was injured," Nichol said. "There had been too many ups and too many downs. "

Nichol always thought that Kostner should skate to "Afternoon of a Faun", a signature piece used by Nichol's British mentor John Curry, the 1976 Olympic men's champion whose torch she continues to carry. "I never thought she was ready before," Nichol said. Kostner wasn't in love with the music.

"I talked to her about the beauty and the ethereal nature of the music, and how I saw her in that environment, in a Monet painting, in the forest where she could be her natural self with nothing put on, because Carolina is a very pure, Zenlike person, who is doing it for all the right reasons."

That was the beginning of Kostner's artistic breakthrough. "Fortunately, she stayed in [the sport] long enough to find out who she really was," Nichol said. "And how she could really compete."

The calming music of "Afternoon of a Faun" (done during the post-Vancouver-Olympic season) helped Kostner's knees stay soft and bending. She had a habit of getting stiffer and stiffer as the tension grew in the program. Kostner was known for her blinding speed on the ice, but she wasn't capable of handling it under pressure and "seemed to explode," Nichol said. Claude Debussy's Faun music served to soothe Kostner as she skated, and help her to become lost in an environment.

At the same time, with the knee injury, Kostner felt miserable that she could not do two of the most difficult triple jumps, while all of her toughest competitors were. Nichol told her: "Let's be proud of what you can do and enjoy what you can do." Nichol nudged her, laying out the idea that now was the time to develop greatly artistically. "Let's use this time, not lose this time," she told the skater.

The wonderful consequence of this new tactic was that, without the high pressure of having to do the most difficult triples, Kostner began to land every jump she did attempt. Her confidence grew as she felt more comfortable on the ice and in front of an audience. It was a breakthrough year. She finished second at the Grand Prix Final and earned a bronze medal at the 2011 world championship.

The following year, Nichol handed Kostner a new task: a piece that started slowly, and then required her to adapt to a quick tempo for the last couple of elements. The music, Mozart's "Piano concerto No. 23," was one of Nichol's favourite pieces of all time. She gave Kostner a CD with a variety of pieces on it, one of them being the Mozart gem, to give her time to feel and learn the pieces. "You always have to remember at their age, these athletes have never heard of an 'Afternoon of a Faun,' or anything of Mozart. You have to give them time to understand it and grow in it." Kostner finally allowed Nichol to push her in this direction.

Nichol educated Kostner about Mozart who was fun, naïve, child-like, brilliant, a tad crazy – sometimes the way genius works. They laughed together over a story about Mozart boasting of a party that he said ended at 7 o'clock and just as his audience thought it had ended rather early, Mozart delighted in telling them he meant 7 A.M. Kostner skated the long program, imagining that she was at one of Mozart's parties. "Carolina likes having little stories like that going on in her head," said Nichol. "She can relate to the music and the composer and she feels connected."

With the Mozart piece, Kostner won the 2012 world championship, her first, and the first by an Italian woman. "To be honest, I think I had already given up," Kostner said.

And she almost did. During the months following her world championship win, Kostner contemplated quitting the sport, but by July, she had decided passion was still driving her to skate. Still, she didn't have time to prepare for the Grand Prix season and competed only sparingly, winning a minor event, the International Challenge Cup at The Hague, before snatching her fifth European title. The 2013 world championship was only her third competition of the season. (She'd won her national championship as well.)

For last season, Nichol presented her with yet another new challenge: Maurice Ravel's "Bolero," music made famous by 1984 Olympic champions Jayne Torvill and Christopher Dean. Nichol had never solely designed a program to "Bolero" in her long career, although she'd helped restage parts of the "Bolero" choreographed by Tatiana Tarasova for Evan Lysacek's short program during the 2008 and 2009 season.

By this time, Kostner was developing an artistic bent off the ice. She had taken a genuine interest in art and music and dance. She studied art history in university. She stepped into a new world where she was as committed to her art as she was in preparation, but now she was doing it all year, Nichol said. "She was listening to pieces of music. She was watching ballets and modern dance and looking at paintings and sculptures… So there was a new level of ownership and commitment."

Again, Kostner had her doubts. But Nichol

impressed upon Kostner that she was capable of handling such enigmatic music. "This tempo will teach us a lot about what you can do," Nichol said. "It's a gradual build, but this very easy-going tempo still allows you to breathe. And let's see if you can handle the intensity at the end."

Kostner had also become a partner in the formation of the choreography. Together Nichol and Kostner – who watched various versions of "Bolero" dance choreography – moved their bodies on the ice, adapting the versions according to their own feelings and understandings. Kostner at first wasn't comfortable with it, shy about expressing facial impressions. As she described it, she had to figure out how to "overcome my shame." Nichol said she had problems with the sensuality aspect of the music. "Carolina is a very angelic spirit off the ice," Nichol said.

Their "Bolero" was much more than a series of moves designed to music. Again, Nichol and Kostner had many philosophical discussions about the many facets of oneself – and that you may choose what you show to other people, so that you do not feel vulnerable. They chatted, they moved, they created, they joked. "We laughed our butts off," Nichol said. And somehow the choreography came together.

Still, the ambitious routine proved a struggle. Both Nichol and coach Michael Huth urged her to try harder, try again.

"Sometimes I hate them for that," Kostner said, smiling.

Nichol responds well to pure spirits like Kostner. She says she does her best work for them. Her purity is almost "shocking," Nichol said.

"Her mother is very similar," she said. "When you meet her family, you understand that this is a beautiful, natural, small mountain village family with integrity and beauty and grace in their souls. You can see it in Carolina when she skates. You can feel it when she speaks. It's something very unique that I'm very grateful to know."

Kostner was ready to unleash this art form at the 2013 world championships, when moments before her name was called, she suffered a nose bleed. Kostner was embarrassed, seeing the blood on the ice. Sometimes it distracted her during her skate. But she did not crumble, like she may have done in the past. She found strength in her confidence, her art, and only singled a triple loop that came directly after a camel spin in which she felt the blood well up in her nose and mouth. In the closing seconds of her routine, Kostner fell on her final move, a triple Salchow, but the nose-bleed had altered her ability to breathe. By the time she finished, she had run out of gas. In that routine, she landed a triple Lutz as if on air, and delivered a triple flip – triple toe loop combination, her injuries behind her.

"She didn't get to perform it the way she knows she can," Nichol said. "There is some business left undone." Still, she earned the silver medal, about 20 points behind Kim.

After the free skate, Nichol received a text from Olympic pair champion Jamie Sale, who blurted: "I can't believe she's smiling on the way into the jumps, she's smiling in the air of the jumps and she's smiling on the landing of the jumps [all with a bloody nose]. How does she do it?"

"She just loves it so much, she can't help it," Nichol says. "She just looks like this bird out there, exactly where she should be in this life, in this moment of time."

Alena **Leonova**
Russia

Born: Nov. 23, 1990

Coaches: Nikolai Morozov, Alla Piatova

Best Result: silver medalist at 2012 world championships.

POOR ALENA LEONOVA. AFTER WINNING THE SILVER MEDAL AT THE 2012 WORLD CHAMPIONSHIPS IN NICE, THE PRESSURE WAS ON FOR THE SOCHI GAMES.

WHAT FOLLOWED WAS A SEASON OF WOES FOR THE GIRL WITH THE "HOLLYWOOD SMILE" IN 2013: TROUBLES AND POOR RESULTS AT GRAND Prix events; failure to qualify for the Final; finishing only seventh at her national championships as a host of younger, talented young women eclipsed her; missing the European championships for the first time in four years; and finishing only 13th at the world championships, the pre-Olympic qualifying event.

Naturally, the voices from back home in Russia weren't exactly congratulatory. Russian sports minister Vitaly Mutko singled out Leonova for criticism because Russia earned only two women's spots for Sochi, after having had three women compete at the 2013 world championships. "Obviously, we expected more from the experienced Alena Leonova, but nowadays there is very tough competition in women's singles skating," he said.

The other two young women, Adelina Sotnikova and Elizabeth Tuktamysheva, both 16, hadn't lit up the scoreboard in the short program, but they bounced back in the free skates, enough that they showed "character," Mutko said. Leonova, 22, finished behind both of them.

"I must prepare for the next season, thoroughly, better, than for this one," Leonova told reporters afterwards. She blamed her downfall on having participated in shows during the off-season, like one in Japan when she "hit the snooze button," she said.

"I'd forgotten that the new season was near at hand, and Olympics were looming," she said. "My programs were made in a hurry, then we had to change one of them. "

Maybe she needed the poor result as a kind of wake-up call, she said. There will be no guarantee that she will make it to Sochi.

Her season was already unravelling when she got to the Russian nationals in December, 2012, and suddenly found her legs go stiff, especially after falling on the first jump in the free skate. Then jump after jump, she felt less in control and couldn't understand what was going on. Even then, she felt the responsibility of her world silver medal. Last season she and coach Nikolai Morozov had focused on using calmer routines, so that she could jump without trying to emote early in the routines. But last year, nothing seemed to work.

The difference between success and hitting the skids for Leonova? In Nice, she felt as if she was confident; in Sochi for the Russian nationals, she'd lost it after some bad results from the beginning of the season that "began to gather like a snowball," she told a Russian reporter.

Psychologically, she was having a rough time, she admitted. Yet her sports psychologist was at home in St. Petersburg, a long way from Novorgorsk, where Morozov had set up shop when he moved back to Russia. Novogorsk is near Moscow. Novogorsk is home to her now, she says on her website, but St. Petersburg is really her town.

Leonova was born in St. Petersburg and started skating before she was even four years old. Her mother stumbled upon an advertisement in the street, calling on skaters to join up for group sessions. On seeing the ad, her mother, Tatiana, recalled a horoscope she had read after Alena was born; it said that the girl would become a successful athlete. Perhaps, she thought, figure skating was going to be the avenue for that success.

From the start, Leonova seemed gifted and shone at the Crystal skating rink, but she was a big fish in a small pond. In reality, when she moved to the famous Yubileiny ice rink at age 10, she could only do an assortment of double jumps, often underrotated, probably because she had been training at a tiny rink that didn't allow her to do more. Her coach, Alla Piatova, a stern taskmaster, worked to straighten her out for four years, while Leonova, all long legs and big white boot covers, soldiered on, working hard.

Leonova finally took the silver medal at Russian junior championships, earning a trip to the 2007 world junior championships, where she finished 12th.

For her silver medal season, Morozov pulled out "Pirates of the Caribbean" music out of his back pocket for her, music that he had used for Javier Fernandez the season before the Spanish skater had left the group. But Leonova and her sunny disposition did justice to the music. She charmed everyone with her joyous finish at the world championships in Nice, France. On the podium she said she couldn't believe it wasn't a dream. She felt genuinely happy for the tearful winner, Carolina Kostner, because the veteran Italian skater had travelled a long road to gold, and Leonova, on the other hand, felt that she was only starting her career.

In her blog, Leonova said she spent three months at a summer camp in the United States with Morozov the next summer and settled in quite well, although at times feeling homesick for Russia. There is a poignant photograph of her, sitting on the sands of a New Jersey shore, in front of a tracing in the sand that spelled out Russia in big letters with a heart beneath.

But she did notice that the atmosphere suited her blithe spirit. "Things are humming [in the United States], but not in a hurry scurry way, like in Moscow," she said in one Russian interview. "And the main thing is that people are smiling. They are not morose but beaming. I'm the same by nature and I've got a Hollywood smile. Sometimes people ask me if I'm American and are surprised to hear that I'm not. It always seems to me when I return from America, that people in Russia are sad and sullen."

By 2009, at age 19, Leonova was also taking part in senior Grand Prix events. In spite of finishing only fifth at the Russian senior level that year, the federation sent her to the European championships anyway, where she finished fourth, yet with the highest technical score among all women. That earned her a trip to her third world junior championship – and she won, defeating Caroline Zhang and Ashley Wagner of the United States.

She went straight on to the world senior championships in Los Angeles, finishing seventh in her first attempt. All looked rosy for Leonova. She slid backwards in 2010, in Turin, but finished fourth in 2011, in Moscow.

Not Leonova. But she needs to find a way to get to Sochi, with so many Russian women competing for so few spots. It will be a furious battle in Russia for those two Olympic spots.

Li Zijun
China

Born: Dec. 14, 1996

Coaches: Li Mingzhu, Li Chengjiang

Best Result: 7th at the 2013 world championships, 5th at 2013 Four Continents championships

THERE SHE WAS ON YOUTUBE VIDEO, WHEN SHE FIRST BURST ONTO THE JUNIOR GRAND PRIX CIRCUIT YEARS AGO, BARELY A TEENAGER, WITH SPIDERY LEGS AND BLURRY ARMS THAT SWEPT COQUETTISHLY ABOUT HER IN AN AUSTRIAN RINK FAR FROM HOME. SHE IS LI ZIJUN, AND AT THE 2013 WORLD FIGURE SKATING CHAMPIONSHIPS, SHE HAD HER COMING-OUT PARTY.

Li seems like an uncanny incarnation of China's trailblazing Chen Lu, an uncommon gem that burst to light at a time when the sport in China was, to say the least, a minor concern. During the 1990s, LuLu, as she was affectionately called by Westerners, was everything a female skater should be: athletic and charming, poignant if she wished, decidedly artistic, carrying her head just so, imparting feeling in a single movement.

After Chen won the 1995 world championships and bowed out after taking a bronze medal at the 1998 Olympics in Nagano, you'd think she would have inspired a generation of intrepid young Chinese female skaters. But no, nobody matched her spark – until now.

Li, the daughter of a well-to-do businessman in the new China, has arrived and her strengths are already becoming clear: she's athletic (She did a triple toe loop – triple toe loop in the short program in London, and didn't put a foot wrong in the long program when she did a triple flip – triple toe loop combo). Her layback spins were things of wonder. And she's a performer, too.

The crowd leapt to its feet before she finished and coach Li Mingzhu – who had been Chen Lu's coach – jumped up and down at the end of the rink, her arms in the air. Li, only 16, finished fourth in the free skate and seventh overall. It was her first appearance at the world championships.

"She is the sweetest," said Lori Nichol, who choreographed Li's free skate last season and who has also done it for the Sochi Olympic season. "She is very pure, but very intelligent and a very curious girl. Very disciplined. She will do whatever you tell her. She is very hard-working. She's emotional, but not in a bad way. She feels things very intensely, but she doesn't react to bad or confused feelings with big drama. She appreciates every little thing you do with her. She just loves it beyond belief."

Some years after Chen's retirement, Li Mingzhu, her coach, moved to California and began to teach Caroline Zhang, an American skater with promise. In 2008, the Chinese federation sent Mrs. Li three little girls and Li was one of them, only 12, and precocious. She could already do a

couple of triples. Also in the group was Zhang Kexin, who finished seventh at the 2012 world championships, at age 16. But Zhang's progress was halted during the past year with hip and knee injuries, which didn't allow her to train. She didn't compete until the Four Continents, and then she went on to the 2013 world championships, where she finished only 23rd. Now Li has come to the fore.

The three skaters trained in the United States for only one year, until the Chinese federation came calling for Mrs. Li, asking her to return and work with the Chinese team. So Mrs. Li signed a contract for four years, up to the Sochi Olympics, to help China's young women learn correct techniques and development.

"I think the reason they wanted me is because I'm Chinese," Mrs. Li said. "For everything, it is more easy. Also with Lu Chen and even Caroline Zhang, I teach them when they were young to go up to the high level."

Little Li's greatest asset is that she loves to skate, Mrs. Li said. She's very coordinated, and she's a performer. "She very enjoy on the ice," Mrs. Li said. "And I think, for the competitor, she has a very good confidence. She can hold herself to stand up there. Psychologically and mentally, she is very strong."

Li's still a diamond in the rough, however, Mrs. Li said.. There is much work to do, like working on her posture and developing a deeper emotion with the music. "She really need to learn more skating with the music," Mrs. Li said. "With good position and into the jump."

Nichol feels Li could be another Chen Lu. Her effort at the 2013 world championships speaks to her grit. "She had a lot on her little shoulders, because she's quite new to the situation," Nichol said.

Now Nichol said the girl must take the next step. Li knows she needs much improvement in her body line.

Li is a gregarious person, a people person who likes to read and to listen to popular Chinese music. Her mother, a former kindergarten teacher, stays at home to take care of her. She has no siblings.

Her efforts at the world championship have helped China get two berths for women at the Sochi Olympics, so she will have company.

Mrs. Li said her student was very surprised to see her free skate marks while sitting in the kiss and cry. She received 127.54 points for the long program which blasted her previous best of 115.91 that she received at the Four Continents in Osaka, when she finished fifth. In the free skate at the world championships, Li finished ahead of Gracie Gold, U.S. champion Ashley Wagner, Kanako Murakami of Japan and all of the Russian women. She was only about 3 ½ points behind the exquisite silver medalist Carolina Kostner.

"When the score came out, she was definitely very excited," Mrs. Li said. "When she gets high points, I'm happy for her."

Her future must be carefully managed, however. At 16, Li is just entering the stage when things can go so wrong for female skaters. "It's very important when they go from teenager to become a woman," said. Mrs. Li. "They change a lot. We have so many young skaters that change so fast. For us, the most important thing is to get through this step and make sure they get through it safely and healthy. After this, their body develop and change and they mentally change, also. And also when they get a little bit improvement, they might also change. In this moment, skater very easy go wrong way.

"We have to be really careful, watch

everything," she added. "It's okay if they improve slowly, but safely. If she pass this step, I think she will be very good. I think she has the potential to be at the top."

And for Li? The memory of a capacity crowd rising to a standing ovation will live forever in her memory. "I try to explain to her that every day you are working hard," Mrs. Li said. "You sweat, you hate, you almost die, because the training is so hard.

"I told her everything is for today, when you look at the whole audience and they stand up for you. Then you feel it's good. And you continue working hard

and develop yourself and get more people stand up."

As for Chen Lu, she's married to Russian Olympic pair silver medalist Denis Petrov, living in Shenzhen where they direct a skating school, and they now have two children, a son, Nikita, born in 2006 and a daughter, Anastasia, born in 2009.

Like Chen Lu, Li was born in Changchun. It's almost eerie.

Kanako **Murakami**
Japan

Born: Nov. 7, 1994

Coaches: Machiko Yamada, Mihuko Higuchi

Best Results: fourth at 2013 world championships, bronze medalist at 2013 Four Continents

Kanako Murakami once compared herself to Takami Sakari, one of Japan's most popular sumo wrestlers. The 19-year-old from Nagoya might have something there.

Never mind that Sakari weighed 310 pounds in his prime and stood, hulking at 6 feet, 2 inches. And frankly, she doesn't look much like the Sakari who used to defy the Japanese penchant for the stoicism-as-a-sign-of-strength thing. While preparing for the heat of battle, Sakari would slap himself hard, beat his chest like Tarzan, make comical faces, and flex his muscles every which way, so much so that when he retired in January of 2013, he was referred to as the Clown Prince of Sumo at home. Fondly of course.

Murakami is none of that. The thing is that Sakari was never afraid to show his emotions. He rejoiced when he lost and bellowed in joy when he won, throwing his beefy fist aloft. His performances were always gutsy. He was beloved for all of his idiosyncrasies. Both Murakami and Sakari were born in Nagoya.

Murakami's mind was on Sakari's heroics (or his histrionics) at the 2013 Four Continents championships in Osaka. Exhausted to the bottom of her toe in the short program, she remembered not only Sakari but 15-year-old training mate Shoma Uno, who used to practice by brandishing his arm (like Sakari) during a jump. It made the jump more difficult, but he would land it. So Murakami tried the brandishing movement too during practice: her secret for success at taking the bronze medal at Four Continents ahead of the more celebrated Mao Asada.

"Is like Takami Sakari," she joked.

Perhaps there is another way that Murakami is like the grand sumo, although perhaps in a more genteel way. This girl is built on emotion and sunbeams. She spills her smiles into the rink and they light up the place. She first barrelled onto the international scene like a sprite on sugar, lively to be sure, not at all like Japan's first lady of figure skating, Midori Ito.

Murakami won a bronze medal at her first Junior Grand Prix event in Madrid, then won the next one in Sheffield, England, good enough to get her to the Final, and just fell short of a medal in fourth because of the vagaries of the judging system. (She was second in the short and third in the long.) That only prepared her for next season, when she won the world junior title. She also competed as a senior at the Japanese

championships, where she finished fifth behind Asada, Akiko Suzuki and Miki Ando.

She didn't lose time when assigned to senior Grand Prix, winning bronze at the NHK Trophy, and here of all places, she landed a triple toe loop – triple toe loop combination. This was back in 2010, when senior women were trying to warm up tri-ple-triples. And with that formidable weapon, she

won Skate America. Yet another Japanese woman had arrived. She took the bronze medal at her first try at the senior Grand Prix Final.

All this time, Murakami was a high school student at Chukyo High School, wearing Asa-da's hand-me-down school jacket and vest. Even though Murakami had lots of her own blouses, she took pride in wearing Asada's old Chukyo blouse too. And she grew into those clothes after three years, when she sprung up 10 centimeters while there.

Murakami was growing up as a skater too, although she modestly said she did not know if she approached Asada in that realm. Enter Pasquale Camerlengo, an Italian-born choreographer who is married to former Russian world champion Anjelika Krylova, now centred in Detroit.

Although Camerlengo had worked with Akiko Suzuki for several years, he had never designed programs for Murakami before. His work with her started with a difference. Her coach, Machiko Yamada, formerly the coach of Ito and Asada, was very much involved with the choice of the music for Murakami. She requests what she would like for the young skater, and for the 2012-13 season, Yamada wanted Murakami to skate like "a strong woman." The discussions settled on a tango by Astor Piazzolla – a mature, sexy piece for an 18-year-old.

"She is fantastic," Camerlengo said. "She is always smiling. She is always trying hard. Of course, she is still a very young girl, not mature yet to express certain things, but she is getting there and she is trying very hard to improve herself."

Her short program, choreographed by Krylova, was "Prayer for Taylor," a routine that was completely opposite to her long. While Murakami emerged in the tango with a black costume and bright red lipstick, in the short, she floated ethereally, garbed in blush pink.

"She did a really good job," Camerlengo said. However, her free skate routine wasn't exactly as he had choreographed it. Usually, Camerlengo likes to have follow-up sessions with skaters to readjust the programs after the skater gets used to actually doing them with elements and jumps.

A follow-up can solve certain problems: Perhaps there is a transition that is too long here, perhaps the lead-in to a jump doesn't work there. But because Murakami lived on the other side of the globe, this wasn't possible.

Instead Murakami turned to a famous Japanese ballet choreographer, Motoko Mirayama, now one of the most important dance teachers of Japan today. Although she is internationally recognized for her work on the dance floor, she choreographed a routine for the Japanese synchronized swimming team that won gold at the Beijing Olympics in 2008. She also arranged a world-wide charitable auction to raise money for the victims of the earthquake and tsunami that struck Japan in March of 2011. Mirayama made adjustments to Murakami's programs.

Murakami has returned to Camerlengo for her long program for the Olympic season and this time, Camerlengo hopes they can both arrange their schedules to work together throughout the season to tinker and polish her routine. He will push for more detail. She will go in another direction yet, he promises.

But already, Murakami has made a name for herself. She's launched herself as an Olympic contender with her intrepid attitude and her fourth place finish at the 2013 world championships. She was the only woman to attempt a triple-triple combination in the second half of the short program, something that was to earn a 10 per cent credit for the first time last season. And Murakami delivered.

And she's growing up. She arrived at the 2013 world championships with a baseball cap perched on her head. Beneath it, everyone could see that she'd dyed the tips of her hair brown. She wasn't allowed to dye her hair as a high school student. But now the girl is stepping out.

Kaetlyn **Osmond**
Canada

Born: Dec. 5, 1995

Coach: Ravi Walia

Best Results: eighth at the 2013 world championships, won 2012 Skate Canada

*I*N A VERY SHORT TIME, KAETLYN OSMOND HAS BUBBLED UP TO THE SURFACE WITH UNDENIABLE SPEED FROM A FRIGID LITTLE RINK IN MARYSTOWN, NFLD. TO GLITTERY WORLD ARENAS, SPOTLIGHTS BLARING. IN CANADA, NOBODY HAS SEEN ANYTHING LIKE OSMOND'S SPEEDY AND REMARKABLE BLOSSOMING SINCE THE DAYS OF BARBARA ANN SCOTT, THE 1948 OLYMPIC CHAMPION.

Osmond isn't very much like the ladylike, prim and proper but athletic Scott. She fills the rink with her sparkling personality, demanding attention of every eye. She's aggressive in her movement, brimming over with joy at every step. She beguiles the spotlight, welcomes it.

The harbour town of Marystown had only one ice surface when 2-year-old Kaetlyn followed her older sister, Natasha, to the rink. Once she set foot in that chilly place, she never left. You could say that you could see your breath in that arena, except that it often fogged up. "I wouldn't be able to see where I was going," she said. But you could see enough, especially when the rink began to fill up with other people. And Kaetlyn wanted to be just like her sister, who is three years older. At first Natasha excelled. Kaetlyn tagged along.

The rink was open only between October and May. Her father, Jeff, an offshore oil worker, was seldom at home. To find ice time, her mother, Jackie, made the three-hour trip to rinks in St. John's. And then, when Kaetlyn was only six, she started spending summers in Montreal to train. When Natasha found a pair partner in Montreal, the family left Newfoundland and moved to Quebec.

In June of 2008, the family moved to Sherwood Park, Alta, her parents both finding work in the oil patch at Fort McMurray. Sister Natasha is now a surveyor there, like her father.

When Osmond moved to the Edmonton area, she began to take lessons from Ravi Walia, who had stopped skating in 2001 after winning a national bronze medal at the men's event in 1995. In that competition, he had tied for third with David Pelletier. Walia won the tiebreaker, because in the free skate, he defeated Pelletier, who became an Olympic champion in pairs seven years later.

After he retired, Walia learned the coaching ropes at the feet of Barbara Graham, whose experienced eye almost singlehandedly turned Canadian skating into a force during the 1980s. When Osmond arrived in Edmonton, she'd never heard of Walia.

Perhaps it was because Osmond never watched skating. She really only began to watch it when she started to become a competitor at the senior level in Canada two years ago. Don't ask her what skaters from the past have inspired her. She won't have a name for you. Now she watches her more experienced peers at international events with great interest during practices to see how they handle warmups, practice sessions, or preparing to skate. Why not look at people like Joannie Rochette at the Olympics or Mao Asada at a Skate Canada? "I don't know," Osmond said simply. "I just didn't feel like watching."

Walia has been helpful to Osmond in many ways. He's a certified technical specialist and has worked at world championships, so he knows the ins and outs of the judging system, what works and what doesn't. He's obviously a clever strategist. And he knows how to live through injuries. He had plenty of them when he competed as a six-foot tall skater, weighing 135 pounds and landing quads.

Many don't know it, but Osmond's path to the top has been anything but smooth. Four years ago, she suffered her first injury, a pelvis that went out of line, pulling her hamstring and her hip flexors to the point that she could barely walk – all from efforts to learn jumps. She still sometimes feels the aftereffects of it. It's no wonder that before she emerged from her middling junior career, she hadn't landed much more than a triple toe loop and a triple Salchow.

Next up was a broken ankle that she didn't know about. At a practice, she landed a double Axel awkwardly on the wrong edge on a foot, which collapsed beneath her. At the beginning, doctors didn't tell her it was broken, she said. They told her they thought she was having a problem with her growth plate. She was on crutches and a cast for three days. She began skating again two weeks later and kept skating on the ankle until September, three months after the original injury.

Her parents, worried that she was still in pain from the injury, had an MRI done on the ankle. The test showed that she had been skating on a broken ankle. "I didn't care," she said. "I was skating." It was a hairline fracture.

The ankle she had injured was her left one, and because she jumps from the opposite foot from most skaters, it affected the landings on her triple flip and triple Lutz.

She also sprained an ankle the next summer, and didn't train at all the summer preceding her breakthrough season, when she won the short program at the Canadian championships and finished third overall.

Her troubles weren't over after that spectacular debut on the national senior level. The following summer, the summer of 2012, she had to deal with a "really bad back injury," she said. Doctors took x-rays and thought she had a stress fracture in her back but bone scans and MRIs showed nothing. Three days before the 2013 Canadian championships, which she won with a Canadian record score of 70.04, the pain finally subsided.

That meant that when she competed at Nebelhorn Trophy (which she won) and at her first Skate Canada International (which she won, defeating world medalists), she was suffering. "I was in so much pain doing laybacks [spins], that I wasn't able to train them," she said.

The problem had started the previous March and continued for nine months.

Now, Osmond prepares for events by doing a lot of off-ice work. The more fit she is, the more able she has been to train jumps without injuring herself. She has a Pilates trainer and a personal

trainer. She does ballet, some fitness, some jumps classes, some zumba (a dance fitness program) and sometimes some gymnastics training.

Walia always saw promise in the fledgling Osmond, who he has coached since she was 10 years old. He saw a young girl who was "very bubbly, positive, excited, very upbeat, and when it came to skating, very driven," he said. "A lot like she is now."

At her first or second competition, he recalls a small girl completely unfazed by nerves. "A lot of skaters were always so nervous or anxious and before they called [Osmond's] name, she kept saying: 'When are they going to call my name?'

She just couldn't wait to get out there. And then she skated perfectly and won. She's always had that."

She always had the ability to turn on the charm on ice, for sure, but the progress of her jumps stalled because of injuries and her results flagged, too. She had won a bronze medal at the national junior level in 2010, but the next year slipped to sixth. She didn't finish higher than ninth or tenth at Junior Grand Prix events.

She didn't do her first triple jump until she was a junior. A year before she won Skate Canada, she was still barely a junior skater, content-wise. She really had only two triples in her arsenal, the triple toe loop and triple Salchow. Osmond regrouped. Said she: "I had to take into consideration that I love this sport and I'll do anything for it."

Suddenly she started landing a triple flip, then everything else came more easily. In November of 2011, she got the triple Lutz, too, and some triple-triple jumps. "What really pushed her was that she was lower [in ranking], than she wanted to be," Walia said. "So she worked really hard that year and came back the next year with all her triples."

After finishing third at the 2012 Canadian championships, Walia and Osmond had a chat about the future, how to reach the next step, where to go from there. His advice to her was not to worry about winning the Canadian championships, but to think beyond that: to get to a place where she could finish in the top 10 at the world championship.

"We didn't settle," he said. "We set a high standard."

Jumps weren't the only key to making the top 10, Walia knew. At the 2012 Canadian championships, when she won the short program, she already had the technical content that the world champion had, but the marks differed markedly. The difference? Detail and performance, he told her. It was important to get every element technically cleaner, with faster spins, more refinement of movement, of everything. He is training her to have no weaknesses.

Walia had been a technical specialist for the men's event at the previous world championship and while there, he'd watched the women's event to see what his own student needed to do.

Osmond has tackled everything that Walia has suggested with gusto, including the mature sexy, "Carmen" routine that made her look older than 17. And with her love of performing in front of a crowd – she skates twice a week at the West Edmonton Mall in front of shoppers – she's becoming an international force. The shoppers now know who she is. They clap when she performs her programs and before the 2013 world championships, they were clapping more and more.

One day, some teenage boys from Newfoundland showed up to wish her luck. They were from a choir, and had been trying to call her. They found her at the mall. The crew of them sat her down in the middle of the arena and sang a love song to her, holding her hand. It appeared to work. Osmond finished fourth in the short program at the world championships, as remarkable a world debut as any Canadian skater has ever made.

Walia believes Osmond has the potential to be tops in the world. She has all the ingredients, he says. She's very level-headed, and most importantly, he says, she has to enjoy herself.

"That's how she got to this point in the first place," he said.

Adelina **Sotnikova**
Russia

Born: July 1, 1996

Coach: Elena Buianova

Best results: silver medalist at 2013 European championship, 2011 world junior champion

*J*UST WHEN RUSSIAN OFFICIALS WERE SCRATCHING THEIR PATES, WONDERING WHERE THEIR FIGURE SKATING MEDALS WERE GOING TO COME FROM IN SOCHI, ALONG CAME ADELINA SOTNIKOVA, A RARE FIND, A GEM, EVEN. AND NOW THAT THE GAMES ARE ALMOST UPON HER, SOTNIKOVA HAS VERY QUICKLY SHOWN THAT SHE CAN DELIVER THE GOODS. SHE HAS FEW WEAKNESSES. SHE CAN TACKLE

the most difficult triple-triple combinations. Her footwork is superb. She appreciates art (warbling over the merits of 2008 world champion Jeffrey Buttle at an ice show in Japan), and of all Russian women, she glides most easily into the code-of-points scoring system, one that the Russians have been slow to embrace. Sotnikova may be the best of the best of that incredible herd of young Russian women, suddenly bubbling up at home, and now striving to outdo each other. Competition has been good for the Russian women. Never have there been so many high-level female competitors among the Cossacks. "The girls are growing up like mushrooms," Sotnikova's coach, Elena Burianova, once told a reporter.

It seems that Sotnikova was always in a hurry to burst forth in the figure skating world. She started skating when she was four, but by the time she was 12 years old, she impishly won the senior national championship – when she was still too young to even compete on the junior international circuit. Skating to "Swan Lake,"

decked out impeccably in black and white whisps and feathers in her hair, she was delightful and surprisingly mature. And at her first senior world championships in 2013, four years later, she was seen to be "ridiculously talented," according to a Eurosport commentator.

Talk about age eligibility for this intrepid young skater? Don't ask. Sotnikova was born a few hours after an International Skating Union deadline. To compete at senior international championship events, like the world championships or Olympics, skaters must be at least 15 by July 1 of the previous year, and on the senior international level, they'd have to be at least 14 on the previous July 1. For junior level, skaters need to be 13 by the previous July 1. But Sotnikova was born in the wee hours of July 1, 1996, which held her back by a year from getting into international events at both the junior and senior level. The Russian federation appealed to the ISU to grant Sotnikova leniency on the rule, but got a flat refusal. This rule also kept Mao Asada out of the 2006 Olympics, although she won the Grand

Prix Final a few months before that. Tara Lipinski was only 15 when she won the 1998 Olympics (and therefore only 14 the previous July 1) but because she had already competed at the senior level when the rule was introduced, she was grandfathered into the big leagues.

Sotnikova seemed to shrug it off. Her mother told her that she was born a month prematurely anyway. Perhaps it was for the best. Sotnikova dealt with a growth spurt and dropped to fourth at her next Russian nationals. She didn't even win the junior event, finishing sixth.

But by the time Sotnikova was old enough to compete internationally as a junior, she hardly put a foot wrong during the 2010-11 season, winning all of her Junior Grand Prix events, including the final (prompting Canadian coach Brian Orser to exclaim to Buianova: "Where did she come from?") Sotnikova took back her national senior title as well and roared onto the world junior championships, which she won over teammate Elizaveta Tuktamysheva. At this level, Sotnikova was already doing the ambitious triple Lutz – triple loop jump combination – something that most senior men don't try. The following year, she was allowed to compete at senior Grand Prix events, but she was not eligible for world championships until the 2012-2013 season.

Atlhough Sotnikova skates daily under the psychological burden and responsibility of being a Sochi Olympic hope, nothing upsets her. She loves to compete, and even to skate last, when nerves can jangle others. She thought she had the European championships in the bag after a strong free skate, but took the silver medal behind Carolina Kostner, who defeated her on presentation marks. Sotnikova had been first after the short program. And it was her first senior international championship event. Still,

Sotnikova didn't feel that the event was anything special to worry about.

At the 2013 world championships in Canada, Stonikova finished ninth overall and left a lasting impression of her fighting spirit. She almost lost control on a couple of triple jumps, but landed them like a cat. And even though she was 16, she sparkled to the soundtrack of mature music from the Burlesque soundtrack. She was eighth after the short program after slightly underrotating a triple toe loop – triple toe loop jump combination and she didn't hold her layback spin long enough, but felt really calm. "To be honest, I didn't quite understand what was going on and that I am at worlds," she said. She attempted a more difficult jump combination in the long – a triple Lutz –triple toe loop but was forced to save it, to steady herself from a flawed landing. Russian officials praised her duelling spirit, although they were clearly disappointed that its three women at the event preserved only two spots, rather than three, for Sochi.

With so many Russian women fighting for so few spots for the Sochi Olympics, there is no guarantee that any one of them will go. Sotnikova and Julia Lipnitskaya will just fall within the age eligibility deadline. Lipnitskaia is a deadly competitor too, with her flexible body honed by an early career in rhythmic gymnastics. Lipnitskaya, the 2012 world junior champion, finished on Sotnikova's heels at the Russian senior championships that year. Although she had won the silver medal, Lipnitskaia defeated Sotnikova in the long program. Her season appeared to be on an upswing when she set a junior world record for the highest total score and the free skate score, all to a standing ovation at the 2012 junior world championships.

With age eligibility, Lipnitskaia is one step

behind Sotnikova. While Lipnitskaia could compete at senior international events last season, her first year of Olympic eligibility is this Olympic season. Lipnitskaia couldn't have made it to the senior world championships this year even after a promising Grand Prix season, when she finished second to two-time world champion Mao Asada at Cup of China, and winning bronze at the Grand Prix in France after twisting her ankle. She was one of six to qualify for the Grand Prix Final in Sochi, but had to withdraw, when on Nov. 28, 2012, she slipped on the entry into a spin, fell and suffered a slight concussion that kept her off the ice for two weeks, and also scuttled an attempt at the Russian senior championships. She did make it to the junior world championship in Milan, and took the second medal behind another Russian upstart, Elena Radionova. Fortunately for all the other Russian women, Radionova will be too young to compete at the Sochi Olympics.

Akiko **Suzuki**
Japan

Born: Mar. 28, 1985

Coaches: Hiroshi Nagakubo, Yoriko Naruse

Best Results: won the 2012 and 2013 World Team Trophy, bronze medaliast at 2012 world championships

AKIKO SUZUKI HAS BEEN A LATE BLOOMER. BUT HER BLOSSOMING HAS BEEN WELL WORTH THE WAIT.

SUZUKI, ALWAYS OVERSHADOWED BY OTHER JAPANESE WOMEN'S STARS LIKE MAO ASADA AND MIKI ANDO, FINALLY WON HER FIRST WORLD CHAMPIONSHIP MEDAL — A BRONZE — WHEN SHE WAS 27 YEARS OLD IN 2012.

She will probably be the oldest female competitor at the Sochi Olympics, if she makes it out of her country, deep with many top skaters who all want the spots. Even Asada is five years younger, 2012 world champion Carolina Kostner is two years younger, and fledgling Japanese skaters like Kanako Murakami are 11 years her junior.

Suzuki loves getting medals, but for her, they are not her prime motivators. She almost lost her career at age 16 when she developed a case of anorexia, when her weight dropped to 66 pounds. Not strong enough to compete, she sat out the entire 2003-04 season. But when she saw Japanese skater Shizuka Arakawa win the 2004 world championships, something stirred in Suzuki.

With the support of coach Hiroshi Nagakubo, the former coach of Japanese men's star Takeshi Honda, Suzuki found her way back. Her first season was rocky. But amazingly enough, at age 26, she made it to the Vancouver Olympics, where she was eighth. And when she won the world bronze medal in Nice, France, she blurted:

"I want to put my medal around my coach's neck."

Medals or not, Suzuki has left a lasting impression: she skates with joy. There is no mistaking it. Her face is lit from within, as if she is the only person in the room. She had already worked with Italian choreographer Pasquale Camerlengo for two seasons when he came up with a brilliant idea for the 2012-13 season – to have her skate to "O," music from Cirque du Soleil. He knew from the beginning it would be a perfect vehicle for a mature artist on ice.

"It's a Cirque du Soleil thing," Camerlengo said. "The music is very flexible to be interpreted different ways."

Camerlengo chose to create a bird theme, with Suzuki soaring and winging and flying, sweetly. His first thought: to call up Hugo Chouinard in Montreal, who is known for his ability to cut music for figure skaters. Camerlengo asked him to insert delicate sounds of birds into the music. "I want her to be a bird," Camerlengo told him.

Suzuki was the perfect canvas for Camerlengo's work. In the past few years, she'd shored up the weaknesses in her skating, so that there were none. She had always skated to strong and powerful programs, and because of her stamina, she could handle them to the last note. "But now she also does the elegance and the glide on the ice," Camerlengo said. "This makes her way more complete so that you can add more variety of things. Working with her is beautiful.

"She is a great skater. She doesn't need many explanations on how to do things. Pretty much what you have in your mind, she can do it."

A skater that Camerlengo calls kind, attentive, gentle, Suzuki wove a spell all season with her "O," showing off footwork that entranced, arm movements that welcomed. Pins could drop when Suzuki took to the ice. Her routine was one of the most memorable program of any women's skater all season, a choreographic masterpiece.

But she never quite got it right, not until the World Team Trophy in Japan, when the rest of the international contingent, exhausted, stumbled their way through routines one more time. Not Suzuki. She won the women's event with 199.58 points, the third highest score all season among women. Only two others had broken the 200 barrier that season: 2013 world champion Kim Yu-Na and Asada.

And the mark is also the fifth highest score recorded by a woman behind Kim, Asada, Joannie Rochete and Miki Ando, a two-time world champion. Asada reigned supreme at the World Team Trophy. She won both the technical and the presentation (program component) mark.

The Olympic season will be Suzuki's last competitive one. Suzuki has a flair for choreography: She understands it and program design may be in her future. While Murakami spent about a week with Camerlengo to establish her programs last year, Suzuki rented a residence for a month in Detroit, to take the time to listen to different options of music and choose it with Camerlengo. Suzuki likes her own abode, however transient. In it, she does her own cooking, bringing a little bit of Japan with her.

Elizaveta **Tuktamysheva**
Russia

Born: Dec. 17, 1996

Coaches: Alexei Mishin, Svetlana Veretennikova

Best Results: bronze medalist at 2013 European championship, second at 2011 world junior championships

Elizaveta Tuktamysheva was tiny, a Russian upstart, a prodigy, a marvel and very, very young when she first showed up at a senior international event, Skate Canada in 2011. Only 14, and just old enough, finally, to compete at that level under International Skating Union rules, she won the gold medal at her first attempt. She battled a nine-hour time difference from home and admitted to a bit of jet lag. Her youth overcame all, apparently, and she admitted to a tiny bit of nerves, but you wouldn't know it. Already recognizing the pressure at home to excel in the years leading up to the Sochi Olympics, she says she just doesn't think about it, hides any knee-knocking and charges on.

She was the first wave of a flood of young, very talented Russian women, precocious beyond belief and taking a leaf from the old United States playbook: girls like Tara Lipsinski and Michelle Kwan who were special almost before they tumbled into their teen years. In Russia, it seems the numbers are even higher. It's almost hard to count the promising young Russian youngsters, and currently there is yet another one, Elena Radionova, who will be too young for Sochi. At age 14, she won the silver medal at the 2012-2013 Russian senior championships. Russia's other women will be happy she's not age-eligible for the Olympics.

But Tuktamysheva was once in Radionova's place. At her home in Glazov, a 27-hour train ride from St. Petersburg on the Trans-Siberian Railway, Tuktamysheva demonstrated that she could land any jump with three rotations by age 10. By age 12, she was said to have trained triple Axels. Spotted by Russian master coach Alexei Mishin, Tuktamysheva started to take that long train ride for instruction occasionally, and at age 12, Mishin entered her in the senior level at the Russian championships. She finished 10th and Mishin got some criticism for pushing such a young girl, but the next year, at age 13, she finished second. Although she was still too young to be sent to the world junior championships, Mishin called her Russia's main hope for gold at the Sochi Games.

When she showed up at Skate Canada, she didn't impress everybody. Coach Frank Carroll, who trained Michelle Kwan from the age that she, too, was a bit of a prodigy, said that he saw a "little girl who has very tiny legs and she can rotate like a bat out of hell," he said.

"She's doing triple-triples like nothing, while these other girls are more mature and struggling

with it." Carroll said her program looked like a junior-level routine, with some "hoochi koochi" moves that were less than appropriate, and that she skated only in the middle third of the rink.

Tuktamysheva has spent her time after that event, trying to attain what Carroll suggested: the mature look. Now Russian coaches like Mishin are looking to western choreographers to give them a leg up on the judging system before Sochi. In the summer of 2012, Mishin, Tuktamysheva and Artur Gachinski landed on David Wilson's doorstep in Toronto. For a skater that is only 16, Wilson said experimentation was the best process, but he found a willing student. He created a short program to Francis Lai's Love Story and a Piazzolla tango for her.

"She's a doll," Wilson said. "She really loves music and she loves to perform and she loves the artistic side."

He found it interesting to be around Mishin, who he considers a legend. "He's a strong-willed person," Wilson said. "He knows what he wants. But I had something prepared and it was really fun for me."

However, Tuktamysheva has run into an obstacle that every coach of a precocious young female skater has nightmares about: growth in puberty. She almost pulled out of Skate Canada in the fall of 2012 because of injury (she suffered a serious knee injury during the summer of 2012) and growth issues. She did come, but finished only fourth.

"She is in the most complicated period of her life," Mishin said later in the season. "She has a 16-year-old body that has changed completely." Most of the time, Mishin said, girls lose their timing on jumps as they grow, although he says he's taught a technique that his girls can continue to do triples during growth.

Still, he said, Tuktamysheva gained seven kilograms in one year, but the girl with the round cheeks managed to do triple-triple jump combinations at the end of the season. When Tuktamysehva appeared at the 2013 world championships, Mishin was no less confident, although he said with a mischievous twinkle, that her goal for the event was to defeat Olympic champion Kim Yu-Na, the 2010 Olympic champion.

Tuktamysheva did land a triple Lutz – triple toe loop combination in the short program that gained almost as many points as Kim did, but that's as close as she came. She spun out of a flying sit spin and messed up a double Axel so badly that she received no points for either and ended up 14th in the short program. She pulled herself together to finish eighth in the long program and tenth overall, realizing that Olympic spots were on the line. Russia lost a spot at that event, and may send only two to Sochi, rather than the maximum three.

On the subject of pressure leading to the Olympics, Tuktamysheva has already found the answer, wise beyond her years. She doesn't read anything reporters write about her, and she doesn't know what people say about her. She just puts her nose to the grindstone and toils onward. And these days, it's a little easier to work. She and her mother moved to St. Petersburg in the summer of 2011, when Mishin found her mother a teaching job.

"I'm just working as usual," Tuktamysheva said. She has competed in the Sochi arena, but seems indifferent to the advantages of getting to know the Olympic surface. "Ice is ice," she said. This mindset may serve her well.

Ashley **Wagner**
United States

Born: May 16, 1991

Coaches: John Nicks, Rafael Artunian

Best Results: fourth at 2012 world championships, won 2012 Four Continents championships

SHLEY WAGNER'S PERIPATETIC UPBRINGING – PACKING HER BAGS SEVEN TIMES DURING HER CHILDHOOD TO FOLLOW HER FATHER, ERIC, A FORMER U.S. ARMY EMPLOYEE – TAUGHT HER TO BE ADAPTABLE. "I WAS ALWAYS MOVING AND THINGS WERE ALWAYS CHANGING," SHE SAID. "YOU LEARN, JUST LIKE WHEN YOU ARE COMPETING, THAT

you don't always have the perfect situation but you just have to roll with the punches and learn how to make yourself comfortable."

Wagner will have that struggle for the Olympic season, of all seasons. She parted company with her long-time choreographer Phillip Mills late last season. And then, her coach of two years, John Nicks, suddenly told her after flying with her to the World Team Trophy in Japan in April of 2013, that he would no longer travel during Olympic season, "It caught me off guard, but at the same time, it didn't," she said. "Every now and then he mentioned that he was unsure how long he was going to be doing this for….I was hoping he wouldn't reach this conclusion."

After all, Nicks, credited with turning Wagner from the "almost girl" to the "it girl" who won two consecutive U.S. championships, was 84 years old by the end of last season. A trip to Sochi, Russia for the Grand Prix Final in late 2012 (with a 10-hour layover in Istanbul) wasn't high on his list of octogenarian pursuits. He'd bought a boat. He just wanted to go fishing. He hinted

after he might retire at the end of the 2012-1013 season, but he'd been saying that for 20 years. He compromised by telling Wagner that he would continue to help her prepare for Sochi. He just won't go with her. Last spring, Wagner spent three weeks finding a coach to take his place on the road – and a new choreographer. Wagner said she wanted to try out a new choreographer and grow, changes that are sometimes risky business for an Olympic season.

With Nicks at the helm, Wagner went from finishing sixth at the 2011 U.S. championships to a victory in 2012, as well as a win at the Four Continents championships, and a fourth-place finish at the world championships in Nice, France, (after being third in the free skate). Last year, she held onto her U.S. title by a narrow margin, and slipped to fifth at the world championships after she and Mr. Nicks decided to leave a planned triple-triple jump combination out of her short program – and she underrotated her double Axel- triple toe loop combination in the long.

"I was happy with worlds, but I wasn't

ecstatic," she said. "I got the job done and got the third spot [for U.S. women at the Olympics.] I'm happy about that, but I think I focused too much on that and not enough on myself."

She knows now that she'll have to have a triple-triple jump combination in her programs for the Olympic season, come hell or hard ice, and it'll be a triple flip – triple toe loop in the short program and that double Axel-triple toe loop combination in the long that she missed at the world championship. (Funny how skaters count the double Axel – triple toe loop as a triple-triple combination. A double Axel is 2 ½ rotations. Compare that to the exponentially more difficult triple Lutz – triple toe loop that skaters like Kim Yu-Na do. Mind you, only three women attempted it in the short program and only four in the long at the world championships, A triple Lutz – triple toe loop combination is worth 10.10 points – and more if you execute it well – while the base value of a double Axel – triple toe loop is worth only 7.40 points.)

"There's nothing more to it," Wagner said resolutely. "I think the key is to getting my confidence with it for the biggest competition of the year. I'll be working out the kinks and mentally preparing myself."

Nicks had been a rock for Wagner, and she left decisions up to him, whenever questions surfaced about playing it safe, or going for the marbles. Now she'll have to figure it out on her own. Still, she thinks she can. Nicks left her with a legacy, she said, so that she wouldn't need him at all for these sorts of things. "He made me into such a tough skater," she said. "I respect him for all the knowledge that he's given me. Honestly, it works out perfectly for what's happened. He made me feel like I can go onto the ice and I don't need anybody. I don't have to be afraid to skate.

I have the confidence in myself and what I'm capable of. He's an amazing man in the way he helps me through my programs and puts them together. He taught me to be an independent student."

Then again, Wagner has had to be flexible. Born in Germany, she moved to California, Alaska (where she won her first competition at age six), Kansas, Washington State and Virginia. She sees it as a positive, because she worked with so many good coaches, learning from all of them. In school, she was always the new girl.

She was only 10 on Sept. 11, 2001 when American Airlines Flight 77 was hi-jacked by terrorists and crashed into the Pentagon, the headquarters for the U.S. Department of Defence, leading to a partial collapse of the building. The plane struck close to her father's office, but he had been at the back of the building, attending a meeting. "That was a really scary day," Wagner said. "He went back and helped people out, but the phone lines were so tied up, we didn't hear from him for a long time."

At 10 years old, she didn't really understand what the Pentagon was, or what terrorism was. "I just knew that my dad wasn't okay," she said. "It was a terrible day."

Her father retired after that. "That was what pushed him over the edge," Wagner said. "It makes you take a second look at what you're doing and readjust."

Her adjustment in the skating world won't be nearly so frightening as she sets herself up to take one of those three U.S. women's berths for the Sochi Olympics. But there will be no guarantees, even though she helped gain those three spots by her finish at the 2013 world championships. Wagner will have to fight for every inch.

Max **Aaron**
United States

Born: Feb. 25, 1992

Coach: Tom Zakrajsek

Best Results: 2013 U.S. champion, 2011 world junior champion, 7th at 2013 world championships

 ISTEN TO MAX AARON SPEAK FOR VERY LONG, AND YOU FEEL COMPELLED TO RUN THE KENTUCKY DERBY YOURSELF, ELBOW YOUR WAY TO THE STANLEY CUP, OR FLING YOURSELF ACROSS AN OLYMPIC FINISH LINE (FIRST OF COURSE), SO STIRRING ARE HIS WORDS.

HE'S A FORMER HOCKEY PLAYER, THE KIND WHO USED TO SET records for penalty points, but he's now playing the figure skating game, and willing his way to victory. Against all odds, he is the 2013 U.S. figure skating champion.

He almost quit.

He's been battered and broken. But he hasn't quit.

Most of all, he's learned in the figure skating world not to let anybody tell you what you can do or can't do. And that is the secret of his success.

He was a hockey player from age four, and didn't take up figure skating until he was nine and continued to compete in both sports until 2008, when he fractured his back. It wasn't a minor incident. He was about 16-17 years old, playing hockey with a wonky back an entire season. He didn't tell his parents, because he didn't want to be taken off the ice. "I never wanted a break," he said. "I always wanted to keep going."

He thought the pain would go away, but one day, doing heavy dead weights in the gym, he felt a little pop, flopped over and realized it was bad. And it was: a fracture of the fourth and fifth lumbar vertebra. It was almost a complete break of the bone, he said. He spent four months in a body cast and seven months in physical therapy. All in all, he was required to stay off the ice for a year. That spelled the end of his hockey career.

He moved to Colorado Springs to flush out his figure skating career. A year after suffering his back injury, he won the bronze medal at the U.S. junior championships, and eventually, the junior title.

But from the beginning, Aaron heard all the whispers and they weren't always quiet. "I had a hard time because all I heard …pretty much through my skating career was that I would never make it big in the sport because I am too much of a European skater," he said.

To him, that meant he was a little too much like Brian Joubert, the 2007 world champion who didn't focus too much on spins, footwork and transitions, only jumps. "It definitely kind of broke my heart, even though I love Brian Joubert," he said. "Just having people tell me that, especially from some top people in the sport of figure skating, definitely really hurt my feelings."

He considered quitting, even up to the year before he won the U.S. senior title. But he didn't. He realized the words had to roll off his back like water off a Teflon shield. He rallied. "I never want to leave anything unturned, and I felt like my figure skating career was unturned," he said.

He knew he wasn't finished, and he decided that if he were to come back, he'd come back with guns blazing and give everything he has to give. "And I'm never going to give up," he said. "And I'm never going to let someone tell me what I can and can't do."

There is no doubt that Aaron is a jumper and a fierce one. He was only 20 years old when he won the U.S. title, but he unleashed two quad Salchows, one of them in combination with a double toe loop and both of those quads were beauties.

Fearless, he backloaded his routine with triple jumps, including a triple loop at the very end, a "so-there" kind of statement. At the 2013 world championships, he was the only skater to do six triple jumps, including two triple Axels, during the second half of his routine, adding to the difficulty and also adding 10 per cent to his mark. Before the world championships, he even played with the idea of inserting one of his quads in the second half, but he did not do it. "I don't want to give up any points in any situation," he said. "I'm trying to give everything I have."

At the world championships, Aaron's technical score, 85.86, was higher than Patrick Chan's and the third highest of the long program. Aaron finished sixth in the free skate and seventh overall, a good effort for a world championship debut, especially for a guy who had never competed in a senior Grand Prix event, and whose first major

international championship was at Four Continents the month before worlds. It was an eye opener for him, learning how to deal with more intense pressures. But he quickly adapted in true Aaron form. "There is no pressure, because pressure is for those who are unprepared," he said. "And I'm prepared for every single event I go to."

At the 2013 world championships, Aaron did two quads in the long program, but he's determined to do three in the future. "And if it happens to work out, well, maybe two quadruple Salchows and two quadruple toes," he said. "Always shoot for the stars."

His is a high-risk program, "but that's what we're training for," Aaron said. He works with a psychologist to ensure that he stays in the program every minute, never letting one mistake foil him, and continuing to attack. He comes to an event well-trained.

He's a math guy. He studies statistics. If anybody knows how to squeeze some points out of a competition, it will be Aaron. He knows he can't make up points in the program component mark, so he has to make them up in the air. He can't see a time when anybody will compete with only triple jumps, like Evan Lysacek did in winning the 2010 Olympics.

"[The quad] is a high risk element and training it every day is difficult, especially when you do many reps, with two quads back to back," Aaron said. Both he and Chan, who had been a training mate in the past, spent a lot of recovery time in the pool and training off ice, lifting weights, loading the back and training the spine to take the impact, and learning how to be explosive out of the legs. Aaron figures his longevity in the sport will be longer than most because of the precautions he takes.

Last year he trained all of the quad jumps, just to see what he could do. He can rotate quad loops and quad Lutzes.

All of this is not to say that Aaron isn't exploring the other side of the total mark: program components. Before the world championships, he made a visit to his choreographer Pasquale Camerlengo for a few days to turn up the performance quotient of both programs. They worked on the step sequences, aiming to get level fours on them, which is not easy (He did). He strived to become the total package. "I definitely think I can skate with the best of them," he said.

And then he said something that truly describes his quest: "I'm going for it all the way.

"After last year, after deciding that I'm going to continue in this sport, I thought, there is nothing I can't do in this sport." Stay tuned.

Patrick **Chan**

Canada

Born: Dec. 31, 1990

Coach: Kathy Johnson, Eddie Shipstead

Best Results: Three-time world champion

IRST THERE WERE ALL THE QUESTIONS, THEN ALL OF THE DOUBTS AND MISADVENTURES. SOMETHING CALLED "CHANFLATION" CREPT INTO FIGURE SKATING LINGO. THE 2012-2013 SEASON WAS A DIFFICULT ONE FOR PATRICK CHAN. SOMEHOW, HE WON HIS THIRD WORLD CHAMPIONSHIP TITLE BUT NOT WITHOUT THE NATTERING NOISE OF CONTROVERSY.

Just as he had after so many of his victories in recent years, Chan had to defend his win. He won by only 1.30 points over a delightful Denis Ten, but that seemed a travesty, judging by the headlines in U.S. newspapers and tweets from other skaters. The 2006 Olympic champion Evgeny Plushenko tweeted: "Denis Ten won that world championship." And again: "Patrick Chan didn't win. His figure skating federation did. That's my opinion as a person who knows figure skating." (Note: If the Canadian federation was really fiddling with results and influencing judges, why wasn't it able to get an ice dancing gold medal for Tessa Virtue and Scott Moir, their prime advertising tool in an event that was held in their back yard? Canada also suffered from a very poor judges draw at this home event, managing a Canadian judge only in the pairs event. Canada had no judges on the men's panel.)

Still, Chan's component marks were met with grumbling. "So what's that odor? Repugnant smell of reputation judging hovers like dark cloud over skate worlds" blared the Chicago Tribune headline, which noted that judges use the program component marks to prop up skaters with reputations. It happens. Canadian coach Richard Gauthier says it sometimes takes a skater a long time to increase a component mark and then, sometimes, the component marks don't decrease as quickly as they should, either.

Still, it's not the skater who should have to defend a mark, like Chan had to do in a press conference the day after his win. The problem lies in a system that requires judges to stay within a corridor of marks. If they stray outside of it, they can be disciplined or at the very least, lose their chance to get an international assignment from their federation the next year. In the waning days of the old 6.0 judging system, International Skating Union technical committees did not agree with corridors, realizing that the judge's opinion that differed from the majority was sometimes the correct one. In the new system, it's rare to see a wide variation in the component marks – although there should be. Gauthier suggested a revamping of the judges' panel: break it up into rotating sections, where

three would be set aside to determine some of the component marks, another three would judge other ones. This idea would also make it difficult to fix the marks, and it would allow for a wider variety of component marks.

Chan had to deal with the system that was in place and the ISU promises no changes at all before the Sochi Olympics. The U.S. media seemed to forget that Chan's win was aided by his world-record short program, which gave him a seven-point cushion going into the long. And after a troubled free skate, in which he fell on two jumps, staggered out of another and messed up a jump combination, he lost the long program to unheralded Denis Ten. Ten was able to defeat him by about five points in the free skate, even though he, too, made mistakes, scaling down a couple of jumps. Ten's mistakes weren't as obvious to the unpracticed eye: He did not fall. Chan was penalized two points for his falls.

Chan's component marks were only 2.12 points higher than Ten's, and yes, enough to give the Canadian the overall win. In his world record short program, Chan's component marks were about five points higher than Ten's. Ten made up much of the difference in the long program, but Ten had lower component marks, perhaps because, for one thing, he does not do the difficult transitions in and out of jumps that Chan does. The previous year, Chan was booed by the crowd in Nice, France when he won the world title despite a messy long program that included a fall.

What did the judges actually see in awarding Chan such high component marks, despite his many fumbles? "First and foremost, it's really something to behold live, to see Patrick move and glide and edge on the ice," said 2008 world champion Jeffrey Buttle, who choreographed Chan's world record short program – and who competed against him when he was younger. "Just the speed that he carries out of nothing. He doesn't seem to do anything, yet he accumulates so much speed." It was a delight to design a program for Chan, Buttle said, because Chan's speed made so many things possible. For example, if Buttle had only seven seconds to place a jump during a certain measure of music, he had no worries: Chan could get up to full speed for it with one crosscut, he said.

"He's unlike any other skater," Buttle said. "Not to knock any of the other men competing out there right now, but Patrick is head and shoulders above the rest in that sense."

And David Wilson, who choreographed Chan's long program last year? "His skating skills are remarkable," Wilson said. "You know those crazy snowboarders and acrobatic skiers, and they just swish and they flip and they come down and they make everything look effortless? That's how Patrick skates. He moves from edge to edge. He careens in and out of everything, with this amplitude. He's been fostering that his whole life."

Wilson says Chan has the heart of an artist as well. "He has this incredible whole package right at his fingertips. His skateability is the best, bar none."

Buttle had never heard of Chanflation, a term originally coined by skating chat-liners to refer to the high component marks that Chan receives despite falls. Buttle agrees that component marks should fall if skaters crash and take a long time to drag themselves off the ice, which affects the performance and choreography. However, if Chan makes a mistake, he has a great ability to overcome it, the former world champion said. "I know with a lot of skaters, the momentum could be killed [after a fall], and the performance is lost and the character is degraded. But Patrick didn't do that. He sticks to the character. He doesn't take out transitions. He is committed to the choreography."

Perhaps, Buttle said, the ISU needs to start redefining what components are. A few bad jumps don't necessarily negate all of the transitions and choreography and interpretation, he said. "To penalize someone for an error, it has to be done on the technical mark," said Buttle, a man who always knew how to maximize his points in the system. "You can't complain about the subjectivity of the sport when you penalize them for performance on something that is a technical error."

People at the highest levels of the sport were satisfied with the results. "Patrick did everything according to the rules of what the ISU wants: linking and transitions," said David Dore, first vice-president of the International Skating Union and a former international judge. "The judges in my opinion reacted accordingly. Yes, other people were seemingly skating well, but did they have the full complement of skills? Did they have the high-level package that he had? No they did not. They may have had some superior moments in their programs, but did they have the full packages?" Similarly, German skaters Aliona Savchenko and Robin Szolkowy won a silver medal in the pairs event after a rash of mistakes when judges met with a tossup of whether or not to rank them higher than Canadian pair Meagan Duhamel and Eric Radford. Dore said the judges gave the nod to the Germans because of their superior transitions and linking of movements. The crowd booed the judges when they placed the Germans ahead of the Canadians.

The flurry over Chan's win was the final sour note on a thorny season for the Canadian star.

Shortly after Chan won his second world title, his coach, Christy Krall, resigned in the summer of 2012, citing a difference in coaching philosophies. As Chan had moved to work more with his dance and movement instructor, Kathy Johnson, on his artistic side, Krall's role diminished. Krall, who helped Chan learn his quad jumps, wanted to be more than just a technical teacher, and Chan was a mighty force, winning nine of 10 events when Krall accompanied him. At the time, Krall was in charge of his daily training and schedules. The resignation took Chan by surprise.

Johnson took over as his full-time coach, but already by September, Chan was peppered with questions: Are you concerned about not having a full-time jumping coach? Could Johnson possibly fill the bill? "I've been doing triples since I was 13 and after eight years of doing triples every day for hours and hours, it's not a concern for me to have someone technically remind me every day of the same thing," he said. Chan initially said that he was fine with the split from Krall, that he was prepared to take more responsibility for his training, which would no longer be so regimented. He also dropped long-time choreographer Lori Nichol for the chance for new experiences with Buttle and Wilson. His first competition under this new arrangement was the Japan Open during the early season, and it prompted more doubts. Chan showed up to the event, unmotivated, unmoved by his new programs and fell four times. "I just didn't want to be there," he said. The results were "like a slap in the face."

At the time, he attributed his troubles to a feeling of "numbness" after winning two world titles. "You become numb to the feeling of accomplishing something," he said. "It's hard to explain." The wake-up call he received in Japan gave him new motivation to return to work harder, he said. But the problems ran more deeply than that. His Grand Prix season was lacklustre. Javier Fernandez won Skate Canada by more than seven points over Chan. Chan found his feet for Cup of Russia, winning easily, but the Grand Prix Final in Sochi – the test event for the Olympics – was a disaster. Chan finished second in the short, but only fourth in the long, managing to hold onto the bronze medal with feet made of clay.

Chan's entire fall season had been a nightmare. He ended the year by taking at least 10 days for a holiday in Hawaii, an unusual way to prepare for the Canadian championships a few weeks later, but Chan said he needed the time away. Finally, in January, he admitted it: The coaching change had not been an issue. The environment at the rink in Colorado Springs where he trains, was the issue. The atmosphere changed dramatically after the coaching switch, he said. The difficulty? He still continued to train in the same rink as Krall, he said. "Figure skating rinks have tons of drama and sometimes that creeps onto the ice," he said. "I'm a very happy and outgoing person. I don't like to not please people, so when I feel like I'm in a hostile environment, it makes it much harder to train."

Unaware at first about what was bothering him, he said he did not understand why some days, he didn't want to practice at all. "I was in an environment that just felt heavy and I felt like I was carrying a lot of weight over my shoulders because of the expectations: 'Is he still going to be good? Is he still going to land his quads even after the coaching change?'" he said. The problem was at its worst during the Japan Open, he said, but after talking it over with Johnson and Michael Slipchuk, the technical director of Skate Canada, his fears were eased.

His trip to Sochi for the Grand Prix Final hobbled Chan as well. Never a happy traveller, Chan struggled with the food and housing in the construction zone of Sochi. He stayed in a hotel with different wings, some catering to those on a tight budget, others luxurious. Chan stayed in a rather modest room. "It was like showing up at "The Shining," with the flicker of the lights in the hallways," he said. Worst of all, he fell ill, attributing it to what he called the "cow food" he ate there. "The food was just awful," he said. "The food was abominable. It was greasy. It had tons of carbs. It was totally not what we needed."

He had the trots before the long program, in which he finished only fourth. Stabilized with Immodium and Tums, Chan persevered, wondering if he'd have clean trousers by the end of the routine. "It was a good test," he said. It wasn't the way he wanted to remember Sochi.

After winning the Canadian title, Chan approached the world championships still mystified by his knotty season. During the entire period, he'd show up at competition as ready as he could be, but he could never deliver the programs. He wondered: Had he trained hard enough? Was he not as mentally tough as he should be? He'd been skating for 16 years and he couldn't understand why he hated the work so much because he doesn't mind hard work. "It's not that I wanted to be a couch potato," he said. "It was just that I had to be in a better environment."

It was a bit of a leap of faith, Chan said, but in the three weeks before the 2013 world championships, he decided to train in Detroit – also in the same time zone as the world championships and a short two-hour drive away. He bunked in with Canadian ice dancers Kaitlyn Weaver, oozing positivity after an injury, and Andrew Poje. "I'm very much the type of skater that feeds off other skaters and feeds off the environment that I'm in," Chan said. "If I'm not very happy or I don't feel that the support I have with the other skaters I'm training with, my training suffers." The Detroit club has a reputation for a positive friendly, family atmosphere. He felt he had supportive friends. "It makes you want to come to the rink every day and work hard," Chan said. "Going to Detroit made a world of difference. It was like the one piece missing in my puzzle." He took a risk and reaped the rewards, an important lesson on the road to Sochi. For the 2013-1014 season, Chan moved to Detroit to train full time. It seems to be working. He walks with a confidence and a calmness now.

Still, other skaters are figuring out how to be competitive with Chan. Chan re-started the quad revolution with changes in the scoring system that rewarded them more, but now others are doing them too – and some are doing more quads than he is. The question of the Sochi Olympic season: Will they catch Chan? Or will he be settled enough to shine as he can?

Javier **Fernandez**
Spain

Born: April 15, 1991

Coach: Brian Orser, Tracy Wilson

Best Results: third at the 2013 world championships,
2013 European champion

*J*AVIER FERNANDEZ IS A CHARISMATIC SPANIARD WHO IS RIDING A WAVE THAT NO ONE ENVISIONED. NOT EVEN HIM.

SOCCER (REAL MADRID), TENNIS (RAFAEL NADAL), GOLF (SEVE BALLESTEROS) AND ART (PABLO PICASSO, SALVADOR DALI) ARE OUTRAGEOUSLY POPULAR IN THIS COUNTRY OF FUN-LOVING, FESTIVE PEOPLE. FERNANDEZ IS ONLY RECENTLY

bringing figure skating to the fore. He has a long way to go, he admits, to nudge out soccer with its dedicated and fervent fans.

Get this: Every town in Spain has a football (soccer) pitch. Spanish children learn to play as soon as they can walk. The Real Madrid team plays in a 130,000-seat stadium. Figure skating? Spain has only 10 rinks, five of them in Madrid, where Fernandez was born. The little rink in which Fernandez first learned to skate closed down years ago, and is now a nice restaurant. Tapas, anyone?

Fernandez's sister, Laura, saw a figure skating competition on television and asked her parents Antonio, (works in the military) and Enriqueta, (works in a post office) if she could join that little club in Madrid. When Javier, two years younger, saw her skating, he went completely against the grain of his sun-loving heritage: He wanted to join too. He was six years old.

There are no private coaches in Spain. In his early flirtation with the sport, Fernandez had five or six, because in Spain, a team of coaches tends

to teach 20 to 30 students at a time. However, luck rode into Fernandez's life with the two to three week summer camps that Russian coach Alexei Mishin used to set up in Spain. Those camps became his only exposure to high-level training as a youngster. Fernandez never skated at the same sessions as Russian star Evgeny Plushenko, but he got to know the Olympic champion when Plushenko put him and other young skaters in the camp through some exercises before they went onto the ice. To a young lad who had already idolized Plushenko, the experience was nirvana, a source of inspiration.

Mishin is known for his jump technique instruction, and before long, Fernandez showed up on the international scene with a mighty triple Axel. Still, nobody paid attention. Skaters from Spain were always an interesting footnote at best, never contenders. Judges didn't always give him a second look either. He failed to qualify for the world championships in his debut season as an international skater. He finished 35th at his first world championship in 2007, and moved up to

30th place in 2008. He finished 13th at a world junior championship in 2008.

Somehow, this laid-back country of siestas and fiestas produced a skater who could do quads. Fernandez himself doesn't know quite how it happened. The first time he tried a quad, he almost landed it. Three days later, he landed his first one, a quadruple Salchow. He surprised himself at the ease and speed at which he mastered it. Obviously, he was born to do it.

During those days of bottom-rung results, Fernandez wasn't a happy skater. But someone was watching. Russian-born coach Nikolai Morozov noticed him at practice at the Russian summer camps, and saw that although Fernandez wasn't missing training, he wasn't exactly setting the world on fire either.

But he saw that Fernandez had talent, even though the kid was practicing really badly. "I don't even know how he saw that [talent,]," Fernandez said. He had been falling on every single jump.

Morozov called a meeting with Fernandez and asked him what was wrong. Fernandez told him that he wasn't happy about skating anymore because he'd lost the feeling "that made you do something." He admitted he wasn't giving 100 percent. Maybe only 10 per cent.

"What do you need to get that feeling again?" Morozov asked him.

Fernandez had no idea.

Morozov asked him if he could come to New Jersey and skate with him, could he find motivation? "Yeah, probably," Fernandez said.

Fernandez had never considered moving out of country to pursue his sport, but after talking to his family and his tiny federation, Fernandez realized it was a very important offer at that point in his life. He packed his bags and left for Hackensack, N.J. a week later. He was 17.

Morozov brought the feeling of excitement back to his skating. "He helped me a lot to believe in skating again," he said. "I hadn't really worked with a big team before, and with big skaters." Adam Rippon, Miki Ando, Daisuke Murakami and Valentina Marchei were there at the time.

With this new experience driving him, Fernandez had a breakthrough international season, at least compared to what he'd been doing before. He qualified a spot for Spain at the 2010 Olympics by finishing 19th at the 2009 world championships – the first men's figure skater from Spain to qualify a spot in more than half a century, since Dario Villalba competed in 1956.

He drew attention for his charming routine to the "Pirates of the Caribbean" during Olympic season, finishing 14th after having added the quadruple toe loop to his repertoire that year.

Fernandez even followed Morozov when the coach moved back home to Russia to work, and that year at the 2011 world championships in Moscow, Fernandez landed two different quads in his long program, and finished 10th.

But Fernandez knew he could do more and noticing that Morozov devoted a lot of his attention to French skater, Florent Amodio and to Japanese skater Miki Ando, he looked to Brian Orser in Canada, who had guided Kim Yu-Na – his first real student – to an Olympic victory in Vancouver. She, too, had come from a country, South Korea, that had little history of figure skating.

"I wanted better choreography, better skating skills, better spins," Fernandez said. "I needed to improve, not just the jumps. The jumps are fine. But I didn't have good skating skills."

He'd seen Patrick Chan's skating abilities and was envious. "I need a small step of what Patrick is," Fernandez said. "When he practices with

not doing his run-throughs, the reply would be: "Eeehhhh. He's Spanish."

Orser called him not lazy, but laid-back when he arrived in Toronto and moved into an apartment down the street from the club, where he did his own cooking. Orser says he got a little bossy with him, pressing him to practice spins, which were not great. In the early days, Fernandez didn't work on them enough and the only way to improve a spin is to practice them until you dream about them. At his first major competition with Orser – Skate Canada in Mississauga, Ont., in the fall of 2011 – he won the short program and blasted his previous best score by about 13 points. But he left four or five points on the table with low levels of difficulty on some of the spins.

Still, Fernandez's best lesson was realizing that he had become a contender at that competition, where he had defeated two world champions in Chan and Daisuke Takahashi. That nudged him, Orser said, into believing in himself, making him realize that he fit in at the top rung. "I don't think he really honestly believed he was one of those guys," Orser said. After Skate Canada, it was clear that he was.

Orser was also intrigued that Fernandez, who had little input into music selection in his first year in Toronto, would only say that he wanted to skate to something "balletic." In other words, he wanted to be taken seriously. No more clowns or pirates. He got "Rigoletto," one of Orser's favourite pieces. Because choreographer David Wilson was overbooked that summer, Jeff Buttle had to finish off the choreography on the short program, and Orser had to design the costumes, something he's never done before. He had to do it quickly, because Fernandez had an early competition, Nebelhorn Trophy.

With all of the support – and realizing

you, you can see how he really, really skates and he just flies on the ice."

Fernandez had already piqued Orser's interest two years before he got the call from a friend of the federation to take on an unnamed skater. (He found out a week later, it was Fernandez.) "I remember watching him on practice and thinking: 'This kid is good,'" Orser said. "He was a bit of a loose cannon, but we're trying to reel him in a little bit."

Still Fernandez, he said, had "such a great spirit" – and he's Spanish, easily charming all of the adult skaters in the Toronto Cricket, Skating and Curling Club. "There's something about that, being Spanish," Orser said. "That's what they keep telling me anyway."

When Orser would call to report to the federation that Fernandez was late to practice or

people were making an ultimate effort for his benefit – Fernandez shone that year beyond his expectations. He'd won the silver medal at Skate Canada, the first Spanish skater to win a Grand Prix medal. He also finished second at Cup of Russia, after winning the free skate, and launched another first: the first Spanish skater to even qualify for the Grand Prix Final. He won the bronze medal at the final, again another first.

He finished only sixth at the European championships that year, and ninth at the world championships, now unsettled by possibilities.

"All of a sudden, he was a front-runner," Orser said. "I'm not sure that he was really ready for it. He got to Europeans and I think he just choked a little bit. The same thing with the world championships. He got a little distracted. He was thinking about that last competition and he couldn't get past that."

But with a taste of success, and with the Spanish economy tanking, Fernandez lost the laissez-faire attitude for the 2012-13 season. He knuckled down to business. He realized that he liked success and to get it, he had to work hard for it.

The dire economic situation in Spain affected Fernandez's skating support during the 2012-13 season as well. Orser said the skater – or his family – was forced to pay for a lot of his own things, like choreography and costumes. "When you have to pay for a program, you're going to work on it," Orser said. "And you need to get out there and get some prize money and do some shows. I think it was a blessing in disguise for him. Now he has to be accountable."

His year of hard work has catapulted Fernandez into a new position: not only a contender for an Olympic medal, but a contender for the gold.

In 2012-2013, Fernandez went from strength to strength, this time defeating Chan outright

at Skate Canada, and winning the free skate at the Grand Prix Final with three quads. (He was fourth overall, after mistakes in the short). And near the end of the season, even though he missed some practices because his skates were lost enroute to Zagreb, Fernandez delivered a stunning win at the European championships, again dispensing three quads with a program that gave officials goosebumps.

Best of all, even though he finished third at the ensuing world championships after having difficulties in the short, Fernandez's winning European score of 274.87 was the highest score attained by a man all season. And it ranks third on the all-time list of code-of-point totals. Chan has the record of 280.98, set at the 2011 world championships. Suddenly, victory is not out of Fernandez's reach, anywhere, anytime. Chan now needs to look in his rear-view mirror with Javi in the picture.

There is no doubt that Fernandez has a beguiling persona on the skating stage. What is it about him that prompts standing ovations and stirs the hearts of judges? "It's a combination of a lot of things: athleticism, personality," Orser said. "He has a lot of charisma and it's the real deal. People just really seem to embrace him. He's a genuinely nice guy. The serge to the top is refreshing to see, and you always kind of hope that he can keep riding the wave."

After the European championship, Orser let Fernandez savour his victory, by telling him to change his flight and instead of returning to Toronto, head to Madrid and "do the parade." Back home, Fernandez was feted. He got to go to a soccer match with Spain's two most famous clubs, Barcelona and Madrid playing. He sat in the owners' box and got to meet some of the players. In Spain, it seems, he's now becoming a household name.

Yuzuru **Hanyu**
Japan

Born: Dec. 7, 1994

Coach: Brian Orser, Tracy Wilson

Best Result: third at the 2012 world championships, second at 2013 Four Continents, 2010 junior world champion

T HERE IS NOTHING TIMID, FAINT-HEARTED, SHILLY-SHALLYING, FENCE-SITTING, SPINELESS, WEAK-KNEED, TORPID, OR SPIRITLESS ABOUT YUZURU HANYU, ALTHOUGH HIS BODY IS AS SLIM AS A SAPLING, HIS FACE AS FRESH AS A NEWBORN. YOU SEE, HE HAS LIVED A LIFETIME BEFORE HE BROKE OUT OF HIS TEEN YEARS.

Before he turned 18, he'd already written an autobiography, "Blue Flames," in Japan with proceeds donated to the rink in his hometown of Sendai. Despite his youth, he has so much to say.

He had been training some jumps in that ice rink at his season's end in March of 2011, when he felt the earth move under his feet. The ice began to shake, the ground pushed up crazily before him, his legs diddered, too. He ran out of the rink, still with his skates and blades on – no time to grab skate guards. He was living through a once-in-a-thousand-year earthquake and tsunami that devastated Japan. Why him? Why now?

"I was sad," he said, bravely conducting an interview in English. "Everything broken and falling. Just scary." His sister, Saya, four years older than he, found him and told him that his mother was at home and okay, and his father, a baseball coach, had been at a junior high school.

His mother was in tears; their home had cracks in the walls. "We have to stop water," he said. "We don't use it for drinking. And the gas. But it was okay."

Aftershakes continued to rumble, threatening more of the same. The Hanyu family had to live in a shelter for four days. Hanyu couldn't stop thinking about what had happened to his life. "I often feel that things you take for granted are not always guaranteed," he said in his book. "Everything exists just by luck."

Only 16, Hanyu's values had changed forever.

But he pushed on. Because Ice Rink Sendai was so damaged by the earthquake, Hanyu had to move out of the area to train. His blades were shot. No amount of sharpening could undo the damage he'd done to them when he ran out of the rink during the quake. After 10 days, just surviving, he had to take time to build his muscles back up.

But worse still, his inner world also had to deal with the trauma of the quake. Always a great visualizer of jump technique, he relived the earthquake, had nightmares, saw it all again in vivid detail. He felt that death was imminent in this world, that perhaps he wouldn't live past 16. He was in fear of being buried alive. "But I want to go and look forward," he said. "I don't want to look back."

The next year, Hanyu qualified for the first time for the world championships in Nice, France. There, he didn't think of winning, he said. He wanted only to skate for his friends, family and supporters. What the crowd saw was epic, so stirring that they stood, cheering as he completed his program and raised his arm and his finger – denoting No. 1 – into the air. Hanyu could not have given more. Gasping for breath (he suffers from asthma) and doubled over to his knees, he bowed and covered his face in his hands at the same time, almost reluctant to leave the ice. He was visibly shocked when he saw the marks come up. He finished second in the free skate and won the bronze medal – at his first world championship. The world knew there was so much upside to this teenager.

'I was tired," he said. "I give everything. After steps, I thought I wanted to give up and stop, but I said: 'Yuzuru, let's go.'"

Hanyu took a big gamble the next year, when he decided to move thousands of miles away from home to train in Toronto with Brian Orser. The motivation? He wanted to skate side by side with Spaniard Javier Fernandez, who had powerful quads. Hanyu wanted more quads, too. "Every time in practice, I want to see that, because Javier is so good at it." Hanyu said. "I want to copy him."

Fernandez didn't seem to mind that one of his toughest opponents was going to learn from his coach. "Sure, that sounds like fun," Fernandez said. In fact, they push each other and pick each other up off the ice when they fall. At competitions where they both compete, Orser wears a neutral jacket.

Under Orser's care (and with more ice time,

which had more than doubled from what he had in Japan, where he shared rinks with 30 to 40 other skaters), Hanyu set a world record of 95.07 points for the short program at Skate America. He'd arrived at Skate America in a scramble. He'd missed his flight, held back by immigration, and arrived just in time for a practice after a five-hour flight. Fascinating: Orser said there was room for growth in that Hanyu could have earned even more points with a little polish – pointing his toe or extending his leg more, or doing his elements a little better.

Hanyu had a tougher time in the free skate and finished third, dropping to second overall, but the polite, hard-working 17-year-old has a powerful personality trait that will serve him well in the future. He never gets depressed about a little setback. He buckles down and trains harder. His biggest hurdle is his physical strength. He lost weight before his first competition of the season, the Nebelhorn Trophy, and lay on the ice for a time when he finished, the asthma bothering him again.

Still, he returned to break his own world record for the short program (95.32) at the NHK Trophy on home turf several weeks later. Hanyu has intense focus. He gets into a zone. He's a warrior beyond compare.

He came to the 2013 world championship to defend his bronze medal but the chips were stacked against him. After Four Continents (which hadn't gone as well as he'd hoped), Orser encouraged Hanyu to return to Sendai for a

couple of days, but when he returned to Toronto, he had picked up a flu that sidelined him for 10 days. Then he returned to training so hard, that he injured a ligament in his left knee, and lost five days with that. Only during practice at the world championships early in the week did Orser notice that Hanyu was getting his timing back.

With typical pluck, Hanyu never considered backing off his ambitious program content in the long, aiming to land two different quads. The quad Salchow was the newest one, the biggest hurdle.

"We did discuss the idea of doing two quad toes instead of one of each," Orser said. "Yuzu said no, because next year he would have to do a quad Sal and two quad toes. He doesn't want to take a step back and I agree with that."

It's just the kind of competitor Hanyu is. There's an element of theatre about this young man, who idolizes Johnny Weir (and Evgeny Plushenko). Only ninth in the short at the 2013 world championships, Hanyu battled to finish third in the long, and touched his knee and his ankle at the end of the program, to thank them, of course.

He's come a long way from his first competition in Chiba, Japan, at age six. His coach had told him to smile. When he stood on the podium, he held the trophy aloft, showing it to the audience. Wearing a childish sweat suit, he was pretending to be his idol, Plushenko, but he was grinning with no teeth. It wasn't really all that long ago.

Brian **Joubert**
France

Born: Sept. 20, 1984

Coach: Katia Krier

Best Result: won the 2007 world championships

AY WHAT YOU WILL ABOUT BRIAN JOUBERT (THERE ARE THOSE WHO COUNT HIM OUT, WHO DENIGRATE HIS EMPHASIS ON JUMPS AND LACK OF TRANSITIONS, WHO WHISPER THAT HE'S FINISHED, REALLY), BUT THE 29-YEAR-OLD FRENCHMAN ELICITS ROCK-STAR REACTIONS AMONG SPECTATORS, STILL.

HE DID JUST THAT AT THE 2013 WORLD FIGURE SKATING CHAMPIONSHIPS as he threw his fist into the air while taking his final bow after the free skate. The crowd stood, cheering lustily at his feet.

Then the marks came. Whistles and boos rained down upon the judges' heads when they found that Joubert had finished only tenth in the long program and ninth overall at his 12th world championship, six years after he won his only world title.

On ice, he may have looked like a valiant conqueror but he had fallen afoul of the International Skating Union's exacting, complex, entangled, crabby rules about jumps. A skater can repeat a jump, as long as it's in combination with another jump, but he can do this only a maximum of two times. (For those who care to try to understand the muddle: When Joubert tripled a quadruple Salchow earlier in the program, and then did a triple Salchow in combination later and then repeated a quadruple toe loop, both solely and in combination, it didn't allow him to do a solo triple flip at the end because he'd already done it earlier in combination. That triple flip worked out to be his third attempt at repeating jumps. Imagine figuring this all out on the fly, with adrenalin pumping to the max.) That mishap for the second triple flip cost him 5.83 points at least, which could have moved him up only one place. But he also lost marks on things that wouldn't have been really evident to the unpracticed eye: doing the first flip from the wrong edge (he'd intended on doing a triple Lutz, but the technical specialists called it differently), and slightly underrotating a couple of other jumps.

The thing about Joubert is that he hasn't ceased to be a heartthrob among fans, and when he launched into his "Gladiator" program with gusto, he was out to make a point. "I want to show to everybody that I'm still here," he said. After all, London was to be the last world championship of his career. He intends to retire after the Sochi Games, to become a coach. He's already been taking some certification courses.

His long career has been one of thundering successes, and more than a few disappointments especially in the past several years, when

he searched for motivation and a way around all the troubles that followed him like a cloud. The Sochi Olympics will be his fourth Games, but his first three efforts have been cruel fiascos sometimes. He was the youngest competitor on the French figure skating team at the 2002 Salt Lake City Olympics, at only age 17 when it was okay to finish 14th. But by Turin in 2006, he was one of the favourites. He finished sixth. Vancouver was a bitter letdown for him. He was out of the running after the short program, in which he finished only 18th, and he could only pull up to 16th place overall. "The Games have beaten me," he said in Vancouver with a long face. "I just can't do it at the Olympic Games. Every time, it goes badly. I don't understand why. I can't explain why." A month later, he won the bronze medal at the world championships in Turin, after having changed his boots.

He's still hopeful. Joubert says he was less concerned about his results at the 2013 championships, than about his personal triumphs: his fire and heart. He intended to do three quads in the free skate in London, but he did one cleanly. He did do a quad-double in the short. And next year on the Sochi trail? He intends to follow Kevin Reynold's path, attempting two quads in the short and three in the long.

But shock of all shocks, Joubert had earned the highest levels of difficulty – level fours – in three short-program spins and two long-program spins in London, obviously a result of his work with Swiss spinning sensation Lucinda Ruh and perhaps even with his unusual choice of choreographers, retired Bulgarian ice dancers Albena Denkova and Maxim Staviski. The Bulgarians had never choreographed for a singles skater before Joubert sought them out before the

Vancouver Olympics. But they also bring structure to Joubert's work (Left on his own, he'll focus on jumps in training). Now the scores are showing that he's improving in areas he had previously neglected.

The story of Joubert's career has been a cascade of injuries, illnesses and coaches. The 2012-13 season proved to be a repeat of previous career themes. He was gratified to be fourth at the European championships, because he went there unprepared. Because his ice rink in Poitiers was torn down last season, he had to move to Paris to train. And in December, he was without a coach at all. He signed up with coach Katia Krier only 10 days before the European championships.

And he'd also been ill. At Cup of China, he had a stomach ailment and withdrew. It bothered him for two weeks, stalling his training late the previous fall. Everything seemed unsettled.

Even if he was not ready for the 2013 European championships, Joubert threw his heart and soul into it. "I gave everything," he said. "I have so much pleasure and fun to skate in every competition. The last two seasons, I lost this. And now I start to come back like it was before. For me, it is very important. "

And don't think you've seen the last of Joubert, come closing ceremonies at Sochi. He also wants to try pair skating. As ridiculous as it might seem, Joubert is serious. His coaches may not be so convinced, but Joubert said skating is an important part of his life and it will do him good to share emotions with someone else on the ice. "Sometimes it is difficult to skate when we are alone," he said. If it becomes a possibility, he'll commit himself to it fully. And it could also lead him to become a pairs coach, too.

Maxim **Kovtun**
Russia

Born: June 18, 1995

Coach: Elena Buianova, Tatiana Tarasova

Best Result: fifth at the 2013 European championship, won the 2012 Junior Grand Prix Final

WHILE 2006 OLYMPIC CHAMPION EVGENY PLUSHENKO IS JUST PRAYING HE'LL BE HEALTHY FOR THE SOCHI OLYMPIC GAMES, YOUTH IS ON MAXIM KOVTUN'S SIDE.

WITH ONLY ONE SPOT AVAILABLE FOR RUSSIAN MEN AT SOCHI, THERE WILL BE A BATTLE ROYAL BETWEEN SEASONED WAR HORSE AND THUNDERING sprout for the rights to represent home and hearth – at home.

But Kovtun appears to be the man that Russia has been yearning for to follow in Plushenko's very large footsteps. Early in his young life, Kovtun languished in all the wrong spots. He was born in Ekaterinaburg, the son of Pavel Kovtun, a figure skating coach (who did not teach his son.) But skaters from Ekaterinaburg don't always get noticed and if they want to advance, they have to move to Moscow or St. Petersburg. Not every family can afford it.

Kovtun cried to be noticed. But he made it to Moscow and got himself into the camp of Nikolai Morozov, a man credited with all sorts of training successes. Kovtun wasn't to be one of them.

"The main idea in that group was he finally get it by himself," said legendary Russian coach Tatiana Tarasova, who has taken Kovtun under her wing like a son, as she is wont to do. In other words, Kovtun was pretty much left to figure out how to become a champion by his own wits.

Kovtun spent only one year in Morozov's group and he showed signs of being a budding talent. He won gold at his first Junior Grand Prix event in Romania, and silver at another in Estonia. That got him to the Junior Grand Prix Final, where he finished fourth. He was 12th at the Russian senior championships, but he also competed in junior, where he was third. His first senior international event was the World Team Trophy in Japan, getting the spot when Sergei Voronov had to pull out with injury. Kovtun didn't sparkle. He was 12th.

But he wanted more and knew his work with Morozov wasn't getting him anywhere. So he went begging to join Elena Buianova (formerly Vodorezova, the first Soviet woman to win a medal in the women's world championship event – a bronze in 1983). Buianova tried to explain that she couldn't take him, because the Russian federation had created a rule that didn't allow students to switch coaches in a pre-Olympic year. But Kovtun persisted. That move proved to be a springboard for him.

It was August by the time he moved into Buianova's group, and Tarasova said they had to start from scratch, teaching him the basics. "He was not ready," she said. "He was in disarray completely. He could not do anything."

He found mind-numbing hard work in Buianova's school but plenty of support. Buianova and Tarasova begged the federation to give him one Junior Grand Prix assignment and he got it. But they had only one week to prepare his short and long programs. Buianova worked on his technical elements and Tarasova worked double time on his choreography and expression, but "very carefully, because he better undertrained than to break," she said.

Kovtun showed a newfound interest in his work. "He understand that nothing comes by himself, and I saw in him immediately that he has become very interested in working hard," Tarasova said.

The group scaled up his technical content and added a quadruple toe loop to the mix. Kovtun won that first Junior Grand Prix event in Croatia. The Russian federation was so pleased, that it gave him another one – but it was only five days later, in Germany. He also won that event, although he didn't skate as well. Still, he had advanced a lot. "I could not understand that it was the same person at the training sessions," Tarasova said.

There were no Russian judges on either panel, she noted.

He was the only Russian man to qualify for either of the Senior and Junior Grand Prix Final. And he won gold by 11 points over talented American Joshua Farris at the junior level. After Tarasova watched him landing a quadruple toe loop – triple toe loop combination and two triple Axels, she could say only to him when he finished: "Thank you."

"It was marvellous," Tarasova said later. "He skated just brilliantly." For Kovtun, he felt as if he was in a whirlwind, spiralling him to heights he had never dreamed. He had done it in Sochi, the site of the Olympics. The win wasn't expected, but still it caught him by surprise.

Two weeks later, Kovtun contested the Russian championships, and it didn't go as well as planned, either in the short or the long. In the end, he landed only one of the three quads that he had planned. He finished fifth, but then the national federation's Committee of Coaches chose him as one of the three Russian men to contest the European championships, rather than bronze medalist Konstantin Menchov, who at 29, was 12 years older.

The decision caused a storm of protest from skaters and coaches. Pair skater Maxim Trankov blurted on twitter: "All athletes for Menchov, without exception." Alexei Mishin, whose student Artur Gachinski missed out on the cut, too, said the decision should have been made on the ice. Menchov's coach, said, of course, that the result was "unacceptable and unfair." Taravosa said that there had always been a federation rule to choose the third skater by committee, and the first two by objective results – and that Menchov and Gachinski had lots of time to prove their mettle on the Grand Prix circuit – and didn't. She was later backed up by Russian federation director-general Valentin Piseev, who said the decision stemmed from Kovtun's strong junior Grand Prix season. And that while he wasn't brilliant at the nationals, he was competing only weeks after his big effort at the Final and probably hadn't recovered yet. (Add to that the fact that Kovtun had to alter his routine, and add 30 seconds of choreography to transform it to a senior from a junior program.) Mishin said the decision of the committee, led by federation vice-president Alexander Lakernik, was only an "attempt to draw in the team Kovtun," led by Russian stalwart Tarasova.

In the end, Kovtun went to Europeans, where he finished fifth, and then he got the nod for the world championships, too, as Russia's only male entry.

Kovtun walked into the fray as if he had the world on his shoulders. He was under pressure to get Russia a second spot for the Olympics and it all came unravelled during the short program. His quad-triple turned into a triple toe loop – single toe loop, worth only 2.40 points. He came off the ice, looking morose at finishing 19th, and out of all chance to get into the top 10. At 17, he was the second youngest competitor in the event, only three weeks older than Pavel Ignatenko of Belarus.

"It is a shame," Tarasova said afterward. "I explain this by a lack of experience. He lost energy in the six-minute warmup. There was no mistake on the entry [of the quad combination] and he just should have done it.

"But I don't regret that he is here. He needs experience. If we get only one spot for next year, we'll send the one who deserves it."

Afterward, Tarasova said that Kovtun had been very nervous before the short program, understandably. And he wasn't the only one feeling pressure. "In my life, my career, I have never experienced such pressure as this season," Tarasova said.

His free skate wasn't perfect either, but he went out onto the ice, knowing he couldn't do worse. It freed him, somewhat. He landed two quads in the routine, and the second one was lofty. He finished 14th in that section, and ended 17th overall.

Because of Kovtun, Russia may send only one man to the Sochi Olympics next year. Russian officials growled about it afterwards. Russian Sports Minister Vitaly Mutko said world championships weren't tournaments just to gain experience. "If you don't have a clear leader, then the sporting principle should prevail," he said in a story from Ria Novosti, a state-run news agency, and one of the largest in Russia. "I've talked about this to the federation management and I am convinced that the decision that was taken is a mistake by the federation and personally by [federation president] Alexander Geogievich [Gorshkov] in that he didn't block this."

Mutko didn't mention Piseev, who had wholeheartedly supported the choice of Kovtun. President Gorshkov, a quiet man, is seen to have less impact on decision-making than Piseev.

Still, Kovtun may prove to be the saviour of the men's program in the new Russia eventually, if not this Olympics, then the next. "He is very capable and talented," Tarasova said. "He has a lot of energy. And a bit of craziness. Yes, I like him very much. He has very vivid eyes, and still a lot of work to do.

"He's just fresh and green. His father is a very renowned hockey coach. He was saying like it was half-ready product. He has very big potential."

His strengths? He has very powerful legs and a very clever head, Tarasova said. "He's like an explosion."

In one year, Kovtun has gone from afterthought to high on everyone's radar. Canadian coach Orser referred to Kovtun as "a little hotshot." Russia has been looking for one for a long time.

Takahiko **Kozuka**

Japan

Born: Feb. 27, 1989

Coach: Nobuo Sato, Kumiko Sato

Best Result: second at the 2011 world championship, 2006 world junior champion

TAKAHIKO KOZUKA WAS WOEFULLY ABSENT FROM THE 2013 WORLD FIGURE SKATING CHAMPIONSHIPS, ALL BECAUSE OF A BAD DAY, AN INJURED FOOT ARCH, A FEW MOMENTS OF UNCERTAINTY GONE WRONG. SO STIFF IS COMPETITION AT HOME ON JAPANESE SOIL, THAT KOZUKA COULDN'T QUALIFY OUT OF HIS OWN COUNTRY FOR THE WORLD CHAMPIONSHIPS.

A rough go during the free skate of the Japanese championships, when his jumps failed him in December of 2012, put Kozuka in seventh place and fifth overall, out of reach of a trip to the world event, the Olympic qualifier.

But Kozuka's quality is undeniable. He's not finished yet.

The 2011 world silver medalist – during the year that the earthquake in Japan caused such devastation – Kozuka is known for the purity of his edge and his easy glide over the ice. He was inspired by Yuka Sato's win at the 1994 world championships in Japan, and the two are cut from the same cloth, both possessing exquisite skating skills.

He was a 2006 world junior champion who hadn't been excessively successful on the senior Grand Prix circuit when he showed up, unheralded, at Skate America in the fall of 2008 and won, defeating Evan Lysacek and Johnny Weir on home soil. He had attempted a quad but fell. But he sailed through the rest of his routine with his powerful skating skills, and suddenly, people noticed.

The year of Kozuka's 2011 victory over earthquakes and tsunamis was his year to blast out of his shell. At age 22, with bashful mien and boyish genius with the skate blade, Kozuka won his first national title, swept both of his Grand Prix events, and his top total score was second only to Patrick Chan's that year.

Backing Kozuka are icons of Japanese skating history. His coach, Nobuo Sato, was a trailblazer in Japan, winning 10 national championships and finishing fourth at the 1965 world championships. And of course, his daughter, Yuka Sato, was a world champion.

Nobuo Sato coached Kozuka's father, Tsuguhiko, who won three Japanese titles and competed at the 1968 Olympics in Grenoble. The elder Kozuka is now an international skating judge. For a time, Tsuguhiko coached his son, Taka, as he is called by his friends.

Early on, Kozuka showed a natural slip across the ice, using the edges of his blades with a natural ease. "He's a skater's skater," said four-time world champion Kurt Browning, who has worked with him a couple of times on exhibition routines. "I can't see how he prepares [for his speed]. I never see how he gets his speed from a step. He can be into the ice, but at the same time, he doesn't leave a mark on it.

"He has gorgeous edges and his jumps are unique. It's in the way he holds his speed and then there's a bit of a delay [in the jump.] I love that boy."

When Taka turned 14, the Satos brought him to Detroit to have programs choreographed by respected Russian-born designer Marina Zoueva to help raise his game in the expression department.

All along the way, Yuka Sato has been his mentor from her position as a coach at the Detroit Skating Club. Yuka has known him since he was four years old. It's a tight family thing, with the Satos and the Kozukas.

Yuka Sato, who trained in Canada, sparkled in the pro skating world after her world championship victory, showing a charisma that was a bit new to Japanese skaters. One of her strengths was to convey emotion in the sweep of an arm and with her body movement.

It was a no-brainer for Yuka to be the one in the family who did choreography for Kozuka, who skated with his eyes down and heart hidden.

She took him to other choreographers, too, such as Sandra Bezic and Browning, Kozuka's idol. "I like to expose him to different people to give him experience and education," Yuka said.

"When he was much younger, he was too embarrassed to dance in front of people," Yuka said. "He wanted to go outside and play soccer, anything outdoors. He didn't want to put his arms up [in figure skating.]"

Bezic told Kozuka that he was an artist on the ice with his feet and blades, not just a dancer. Her advice triggered something in him. And Browning showed Kozuka some fun. He took him to a karaoke bar, got him to relax, got him to exude. It's all part of the game in figure skating.

Kozuka's progress has warmed Yuka's heart. "It's very cool to see somebody grow up," she said.

Evan **Lysacek**
United States

Born: June 4, 1985

Coach: Frank Carroll

Best Result: 2010 Olympic champion, 2009 world champion

ONE LESSON 2010 OLYMPIC CHAMPION EVAN LYSACEK HAS TO LEARN: THAT HE'S MADE OF FLESH AND BONE, AND NO MORE THAN THAT.

HIS WILL AND DESIRE HAVE NEVER BEEN IN DISPUTE.

IT COULD BE SAID THAT HIS WILL CARRIED HIM TO THE TOP OF THE PODIUM AT THE VANCOUVER OLYMPICS FOUR YEARS AGO. INFLAMMATION OF

tendons and ligaments in his left foot hobbled his quad attempts at the 2009 world championships and he took at least a month off to give the injury time to heal. But during Olympic season, Lysacek had to deal with foot problems, still. He actually finished only second at the U.S. nationals (and third in the free skate) with an underrotated quad. Then he broke his foot and training the quad became a risk. Coming to the Vancouver Olympics, he decided to "lay off that pressure on the left foot and try to make it through these Games successfully."

Without a quad, he maximized his points on other elements, and won by 1.31 points with an air of ferocity. He hadn't expected the medal.

Lysacek took the first year off after the Olympics to do such things as finish second in the popular television show, "Dancing with the Stars," and apply himself to his multitude of charities, but the next year, the American star eventually announced he intended to defend his Olympic title at Sochi. However, a dispute with the United States Figure Skating federation scuttled the

2011-12 season. And injuries decimated the 2012-13 season.

Lysacek was set to compete at Skate America in Kent, Washington in October of 2012 – which would have been his first competition since the Olympic Games – but he withdrew after aggravating a groin injury. He admitted it was his fault. He trains too hard. Perhaps, he had pushed things a little too hard, a little too soon after being injured, he said.

He originally sustained the injury in early August, and was off the ice for about five weeks after his leg slipped on some gravel while he was doing a lunge to warm up for practice. He kept skating on it for a few days until he couldn't walk.

He also ended up missing the U.S. championships in Omaha, after undergoing surgery in November of 2012 to repair a torn muscle in his lower abdomen – basically a sports hernia. The sports hernia had been diagnosed during an assessment of his groin injury. That injury put him off ice for six weeks. He did return and began training again, but thought he needed

another three weeks to be in top shape for the U.S. championships, so he withdrew.

"I won't give up," he tweeted. The upside of his time off? It's given his body time to heal.

Although he's been away from competition, he'd been paying attention, watching Japanese, Canadian and European skaters. Knowing about the escalation of quads since the Vancouver Games, Lysacek has been working on two quads. "I'm going to be back, man," he said.

His other motivation? He wants to help the United States to win the first figure skating team medal offered at the Games.

He's already had his routines choreographed by Lori Nichol, but in early spring had been wavering about using the short program for the Olympics. Clearly, he's intent on coming back. "He's very excited these days," Nichol said. "He's feeling much better. The biggest lesson for him is having to finally learn not to overwork. But he's optimistic."

Unfortunately, by early September, 2013, Lysacek was dealing with injury again. He had to withdraw from the U.S. International Classic in Salt Lake City in mid-September with a slight abdominal tear that wasn't serious enough to keep him away from a Sochi bid. Still, it's a setback in a year in which setbacks are worrisome.

Not long after Nichol had choreographed the routines during the spring of 2012, Lysacek was "on fire," she said, unleashing a quadruple toe – half loop – triple flip combination during training – when he wasn't injured. (He'll need a quad in his 2014 Olympic season, although he still maintains that skating cleanly is the key.) And he showed more artistic commitment than he'd had in the past.

"I had said to him, what's the point, if you're not interested, and you're just going to be cautious and do 70 per cent of what you can do?" Nichol said. "If you're willing to do 150 per cent, I'm on."

Lysacek bought into Nichol's challenge. He began to skate with passion, she said. And he wasn't afraid to expend the energy emotionally and physically to portray the character and music any more – a breakthrough for him. "Hopefully he can be healthy enough to show everyone that," Nichol said.

If Lysacek were to win the Sochi Games, he'd become the first man in 62 years to repeat an Olympic win. Dick Button scored a double in 1948 and 1952. As it was, Lysacek became the first American in 24 years to win Olympic gold in men's figure skating in 2010, the previous one being Brian Boitano in 1988.

Evgeny **Plushenko**
Russia

Born: Nov. 3, 1982

Coach: Alexei Mishin

Best Result: 2006 Olympic champion, three-time world champion, most recently in 2004

THE STORIES ABOUT EVGENY PLUSHENKO OVER THE PAST TWO YEARS HAVE SWIRLED AROUND HIS AGING BODY, BATTERED BY THE POUNDING OF A HUNDRED QUADS.

IT IS THE DREAM OF THE 2006 OLYMPIC CHAMPION FROM RUSSIA TO MAKE IT TO HIS FOURTH OLYMPIC GAMES – IN HIS HOME COUNTRY NO LESS, BUT HE'S BEEN hobbled by his body. By the time of the Sochi Games, he will be 31 years old, a father, a former politician, a husband, a guy who's trying to keep his household together.

He's competed only sparingly since winning an Olympic silver medal at the Vancouver Games, a controversy only by his assertion that the winner, Evan Lysacek, was less than an Olympic champion because he didn't include a quad in his routine.

Last year, quads, even triple Axels, have escaped Plushenko.

But the spirit is willing. Perhaps too willing sometimes.

He was forced to withdraw after the short program at the 2013 European championships in Zagreb, Croatia, out of business with back pains that had bothered him for a year. Four months before that, he'd been ready – he'd been landing two different quads at the Russian test skate at the start of the season. Afterward, Plushenko admitted he had attempted too many quad jumps too early in the season. He'd been landing quad Salchows and was even trying quad Lutzes. Higher, faster, stronger, that's the Plushy everyone knows. But his body is not young any more.

That heavy workload aggravated a spinal condition and off he went to Munich for emergency surgery, treatment of a disc hernia. He wasn't supposed to have done anything for 10 days, but he was back on the ice in seven. Actually, the doctors had told him to stay off the ice for a month, but Plushenko couldn't stay away, feeling pressure to be ready for the Russian championships. He not only went back too soon, but he went at his training with intense gusto. That was his first mistake.

Because of this, complications arose and he went for an injection to ease the pain, a nerve block, in St. Petersburg, where he trains. This didn't solve the problem, however, and Plushenko admitted to reporters that he was reduced to tears in practices because he could not even do simple triple jumps. He said he felt like giving up.

Plushenko did compete at the Russian championships after difficult preparation, and won

his 10th national title in Sochi. He won by 12 points. But he skated through pain to land a two-footed quadruple toe loop, two triple Axels, and four other triples. He had only the second highest technical score of the long program although he had presented a simplified version of the long program (the more complicated one had two quads) and he wasn't able to sleep the night before. Ominously, an earthquake made all the hangers in his room rattle. It didn't help his nerves.

Plushenko knew he needed a miracle, that that performance wouldn't win him a medal at the European championships in Zagreb. And that was his second major mistake: competing at the European championships. During the short program, he crashed on a triple Axel, a fall he did not attribute to his injury. Yet all the same, he withdrew, in tears. Even his coach Alexei Mishin noted later that he should not have competed because the disc was in such bad condition.

A short time later on Jan. 31, 2013, Plushenko underwent back surgery in Tel Aviv, Israel to remove one of his spinal discs and replace it with a synthetic one. Russian television cameras followed him there.

The recovery? Plushenko had to be willing to be patient with this one, because the mending period wasn't to be short. Still, Mishin said he'd still be able to walk and swim about four weeks after the surgery.

All of this, and never mind that he underwent surgery on a knee the previous February to clean out his meniscus, just to be able to return.

It seems now that Plushenko's ability to win a medal in Sochi is a long shot. But everyone said that about him when he made his comeback for the Vancouver Games. His progress from the beginning of the year to the Games was miraculous. By late July, 2013, after being off the ice for four months, Plushenko landed his first triple Axel since surgery, and by August, he was landing quads. He promises not to overdo things.

The mop-haired blond Russian, the son of a carpenter rom the industrial city of Volgograd in eastern Russia, had to leave for St. Petersburg when he was 11 because his rink closed down. He became the poster child of Alexei Mishin's jumping technique and at age 14, became the youngest victor of the world junior championships. The next year, he won the bronze medal at the 1998 senior world championships.

In all, Plushenko has won three world titles, an Olympic gold and two Olympic silver medals. He was the first to perform a quadruple toe loop – triple toe loop – double loop in competition (at the 1999 NHK Trophy), and also the first to make that combination a quad-triple-triple, too (2002 Cup of Russia.) Somebody has estimated that he has done about 100 quads in his career. He had a brief political career, elected to the St. Petersburg legislature for the A Just Russia party, in 2007, but came under fire for having poor attendance. He left politics in December of 2011.

On September 12, he married record producer Yana Rudkovskaya, who supports his skating career. They had a son, Alexander in January, 2013. Plushenko also has a son from a previous marriage.

When he's finished with his competitive career, he intends to establish another skating school in St. Petersburg to keep the Russian tradition of excellence in skating alive.

Kevin **Reynolds**

Canada

Born: July 23, 1990

Coach: Joanne McLeod

Best Result: won the 2013 Four Continents championship, fifth at the 2013 world championship

THERE WERE THOSE WHO THOUGHT KEVIN REYNOLDS WAS A LITTLE DELIRIOUS WHEN HE DECLARED HIS GOAL FOR THE 2012-2013 SEASON: TO FINISH IN THE TOP SIX AT THE WORLD FIGURE SKATING CHAMPIONSHIPS. THE PORT COQUITLAM, B.C., SKATER HADN'T FINISHED BETTER THAN 11TH AT THE WORLD CHAMPIONSHIPS (AND THAT WAS FOUR YEARS PREVIOUSLY),

had never won a Grand Prix medal, and hadn't finished higher than third at the Canadian championships (in 2010). That third place finish at the national championship had left him off the Olympic team in Vancouver in his home turf. He had to watch from the stands, on the outside looking in.

So what could 22-year-old Reynolds be thinking by planning such a seemingly overzealous target?

Under the radar, always underrated, Reynolds astonished the world by winning the Four Continents championships in Osaka in February of 2013, dusting off all the top skaters from the United States, and even more startlingly from Japan (on their own country), including a world champion. And then he continued on to the 2013 world championships and finished fifth, after being third in the short program.

And along the way, he'd finished second at the 2013 Canadian championships, with a wildly higher free skate technical score than two-time world champion Patrick Chan, better by 12.64

points. For the first time, Reynolds had landed three fully rotated quads in the long program. His technical mark in the free was higher than that of Javier Fernandez when he won the European title with three quads. And Reynolds recorded a final score of 261.26, that was 40 points higher than his international record. Overall he had landed five quads at the event, a tough act for anybody to follow. And finally, he was nudging Chan like no Canadian had ever nudged him before: Reynolds was only 3.18 points behind him in the end at the national event. Has Reynolds finally made believers out of doubters?

Coach Joanne McLeod always thought Reynolds had it in him to tangle with the best as long as he could unfurl his inner artist and improve his program component (presentation) marks. And she knew just the person who could help: former world ice dancing champ Shae-Lynn Bourne, perhaps one of the greatest female skaters to ever set foot on a frozen pond, so deft were her feet, so unquestioned was her flair for the feeling of music.

McLeod didn't want Bourne to stick around for a season or two. She wanted her to guide Reynolds long-term, to get him to the Sochi Games. "She wanted people to see his personality," Bourne said. "She thought there was a lot inside of him, but no one was seeing it."

When Bourne first worked with Reynolds, she found that the skater had a feel for music and its rhythm: a good start. He could pick up a beat easily. Reynolds was enthusiastic about every door Bourne opened and soaked it up like a sponge.

As his work improved, so did his confidence, Bourne said. "When you start to be present and show yourself, it builds your confidence and everything works. In the last couple of years, people have started to enjoy him. He's made people smile. He's left them with a good feeling and everything connects."

As fast as Reynolds was in the air, rotating four times in a flash, he was also quick on the ice with his feet. The first year that Bourne worked with him, she gave him a jazz program, because she could see he was light on his feet and quick. "He twizzles fast, too, and I thought since he had this sense of music, he could be like the instrument. And he has this smirk when he does things. There's this little playful boy and I just wanted to grab hold of that."

The more he puts himself into his skating, the more he lights up, Bourne said. And whenever they got to the footwork sections, Reynolds was clearly eager. "He'd be excited and ready to take it on," she said. "I'd make something and I'm always asking: 'Is that too hard?' and he would say: 'Give me more, give me more.' He likes the fast steps and the quick, difficult moves. He comes alive as it gets more intricate."

How did she make Reynolds come out of his

shell? "I think people need to hear when they do things well," she said. "I think he's been told so often that he doesn't have style, and you start to believe that. I'm a firm believer that you can kind of do whatever you want and it's really what you believe that can change the outcome."

It doesn't matter how accomplished a skater you are, Bourne reasoned, or how technically good you are, it will mean nothing if you don't touch people. "It sets you apart," Bourne said.

Of course, Reynolds has all of the records, the ones that made people take notice in the beginning: He was the first Canadian to land a quad-triple-triple jump combination (2008 Canadian championships); the first skater to land two quads in a short program (2010 Skate Canada Grand Prix); and first Canadian man to do three quads in the free skate (2013 Canadian championships). He landed his first quad (a Salchow) at age 15, and has flirted with doing a quad loop in competition, but has never landed it.

He's a highly intelligent young man, the one who can answer any question about all of the International Skating Union scoring intricacies and rules. Fascinated by Japanese culture – and he's amassed leagues of fans in Japan – Reynolds is learning how to speak Japanese. Last year, he asked Japanese skater Kenji Miyamoto, a retired Japanese champion ice dancer, to design his free skate. It was a unique choice. Miyamoto hadn't done a lot of routines for western skaters and his English wasn't stellar. "I liked what he did with Takahashi during the [Vancouver] Olympic season," Reynolds said. "His programs are very different, in terms of movement. It's very lyrical and flowing and that contrasted to what I did in the past. I haven't been able to do it in the past. I was nervous at the start of the season, thinking I wouldn't be able to handle it, with some of the jumps not going as planned."

But it came together, and crowds began to see the full effect of the Miyamoto-Bourne influence on Reynolds by years' end. For Olympic season, Reynolds has turned to Lori Nichol for the first time for his long program.

Ice dancers have been Reynolds' salvation. He has also worked on stroking and edges with Canadian ice dancers-turned-coaches Megan Wing and Aaron Lowe. But Bourne has been a "magical" influence, MacLeod says. "Music is her soul. She has a magical ability to entertain or sooth or bring you in when she skates. I think that is exactly what Kevin needed and I feel that choice was the biggest change in the direction to his success."

Daisuke **Takahashi**
Japan

Born: Mar. 16, 1986

Coach: Utako Nagamitsu, Takeshi Honda, Nikolai Morozov

Best Results: 2010 world champion, 2010 Olympic bronze medalist

AISUKE TAKAHASHI IS A MAN OF FASHION, OF STYLE, OF ART. HE'S A SNAPPY DRESSER. HE HAS INPUT INTO HIS OWN COSTUME DESIGN. EVERY TIME YOU SEE HIM, DAI-SAN SPORTS A NEW HAIRSTYLE.

TAKAHASHI IS THE CONSUMMATE ENTERTAINER, HIS FIRST GOAL TO "GRAB THE HEARTS" OF SPECTATORS. BUT HE'S ALSO BEEN AN IMPORTANT

trailblazer for men's skating in Japan – the first Japanese man to win a world figure skating title (2010) and the first Japanese figure skater to win an Olympic medal (bronze in 2010), so much so that an entire generation of intrepid, high-flying Japanese males now dominate the sport. And those who came after Takahashi may keep him from the Sochi Olympics. Although he has set world record scores in the past, and still holds a trio of top-three all-time scores for short program, long program and total, Takahashi himself will say that he doesn't even know if he will qualify out of his country, so deep is the talent. Humble and unaffected by his successes, Takahashi is widely loved – by fans and other skaters.

Men's skating in Japan wasn't nearly as popular as it is now when Takahashi took to the ice in the small Japanese city of Kurashiki, where his father works in construction with very high scaffolding, like bridges, and his mother a hair stylist in a little modest barber shop. According to a Japanese television documentary of Takahashi's life, he was a quiet, shy boy and his parents wanted

to expose him to a sport. His father had been a track and field athlete, and his brothers were in martial arts. Takahashi continued to turn down all sporting suggestions until his family took him to an ice hockey rink. "No way. I can't do that," he said and then spied an ice surface with figure skaters on it. That got him.

Takahashi was the youngest son of four boys, but his mother had wished for a girl, the documentary said. She wheeled him into figure skating classes, often made up entirely of girls. His father sharpened his blades himself, and Takahashi showed up in competitions with home-made costumes and home-made choreography. He won his first competition.

His parents had no idea that figure skating would cost so much. Friends stepped in to help. While his mother was working, Hideko Hatsuse, a woman who also worked in the shop, would shuttle Takahashi to the rinks. When he finished skating at one spot, she'd take him to another. She also created a help system: leaving a large plastic bottle on the front counter of the shop

where patrons deposited coins to help finance Takahashi's career. With the community behind him, Takahashi won the world junior championship in 2002, the first and only time he competed in it.

By chance, while he was a junior skater at a training camp in Sendai, he bumped into Utako Nagamitsu, a coach that could teach him expression, he thought. The relationship between the two has been binding and powerful. She's still with him. It's not hard to understand why. When Takahashi had to move away from Kurashiki to continue his skating at a higher level, Nagamitsu took him into her home and cooked for him.

His senior career didn't start out with a bang, more like a whimper. His results were inconsistent. Takeshi Honda was the star. When Honda was forced to with draw with an injury from the 2005 world championships, it fell upon Takahashi's shoulders to qualify spots for the 2006 Olympics. He finished only 15th, and got only one spot for Japan. Takahashi got the call for the Olympics, and finished eighth after a poor free skate.

At one point, he almost quit. But he continued and ended up winning a silver medal at the 2007 world championships in Tokyo, the first silver for a Japanese man at a world championship. His star status was sealed.

However, Takahashi missed his entire 2008-2009 season when, during a practice on Oct. 21, 2008, he fell attempting a triple Axel and tore the anterior cruciate ligament in his right knee. Surgery repaired the ligament damage and doctors inserted a bolt that was removed three years later. Nine hours a day of excruciating rehabilitation exercises drove him to depression. At one point, according to the Japanese documentary, Takahashi suddenly went missing. His coach

lost contact with him – he had still been living in her house. He just didn't come home. Ten days later, Nagamitsu returned home and found Takahashi's shoes at the door. He was in bed. She told him that if he wanted to quit, it would be okay, she would take it upon herself to apologize for his retirement. But something – maybe her words – lit a fire under Takahashi and back he went to rehab.

Not that it was easy. When he finally began practicing jumps the following June, he was humbled. He could not jump at all. He had to work his muscles back into competition form. Months later, he won the Finlandia Trophy and then eventually the Japanese championships. Seven months after he returned to the ice, he won the Olympic bronze medal, then a gold at the world championships. Strangely enough, it was one of his best years. He had triumphed over himself.

Because a drastic injury has a way of changing a mindset, Shae-Lynn Bourne, who choreographed his free skate to "I, Pagliacci," for the 2012-2013 season, said she felt that Takahashi's skating had improved since his injury, although as Takahashi said, it caused him to lose his quad. He now fumbles the quad jump more often than he lands it. "The quad has never come back," he said.

"That injury at that time of his life made a huge difference to him," Bourne said. "He took ownership of himself. Sometimes when you come out of the bubble – we're all in a bubble of some sort – you're forced to look at your life from the outside. When he did start to skate, he was doing it for himself, on his own. I think it made him a much stronger person and it showed in his skating. He started skating with a different kind of confidence. It's not like he was told what to do, but he was making it happen."

beginning to end and he could do everything that I asked him and beyond."

Last season, Takahashi didn't come to Bourne until very late – August of 2012 – and when the Japanese skater told her he wanted to skate to classical music that was emotional and passionate, Bourne first thought of the Pagliacci music by Ruggero Leoncavallo. She presented Takahashi with two or three choices, and he picked the Pagliaccci theme "without a blink," she said.

He showed the program at Japan Open only two weeks after Bourne had choreographed it for him – and he won. "He really skates with such a sensitivity to the ice with his blades and he has such a beautiful heart," Bourne said. "He listens and does anything that you ask him to do. He feels music."

And he's never content. Takahashi always pushes himself as an artist, learning from everyone. At one point, he went to France to work with ice dancing coach Muriel Zazoui and Olivier Schoenfelder, because he always respected Schoenfelder's work on the ice. Every year, he tries a new choreographer. "Not all competitors will do that," Bourne said. "They'll go with what's safe or what feels comfortable. He's always going out of the box."

And for the year leading up to the Olympics, Takahashi will find his choices more important than any other year. His two Olympic routines will be the last two he'll do in competition. He wants no regrets. For the short program, he will skate to "Sonatina for Violin," composed by Mamoru Samuragochi, who is deaf in both ears; Takahashi says the music inspires hope. For the long, it's a Beatles medley, for which he's using Canadian choreographer Lori Nichol for the first time.

Takahashi has said he's retiring after Sochi. He'll leave a big hole when he goes.

Bourne had earlier choreographed a short program for Takahashi in the 2010-2011 season to mambo music and "I had the time of my life," she said. "Whenever you get a great skater who can do everything, it's exciting because there is no limit. It was fun music and he danced from

Denis **Ten**
Kazakhstan

Born: June 13, 1993

Coach: Frank Carroll

Best Result: second at the 2013 world championship, world junior champion in 2006

Y WINNING A SURPRISE SILVER MEDAL AT THE 2013 WORLD FIGURE SKATING CHAMPIONSHIPS IN LONDON, ONT., DENIS TEN BECAME A POSTER BOY FOR MANY THINGS: ILLUSTRATING HOW WELL THE (RELATIVELY NEW) JUDGING SYSTEM WORKS WHEN IT ENABLES AN OUTSIDER TO BOUNCE TO THE TOP OF THE STANDINGS; HOW IT'S POSSIBLE FOR A skater from a country with no history of the sport to turn into an Olympic contender; how no one should give up, no matter how bad things seem in the arena of winning and losing.

Ten, the first skater from Kazakhstan to do anything in figure skating, including most recently, win a world medal, hadn't exactly set the world on fire during his 2012-13 season, finishing near the bottom of the heap with sixth and ninth-place finishes at his two Grand Prix events. And he'd finished only 17th in the long program at the Four Continents championships in Osaka, Japan, after falling twice and doubling three jumps. He had never won a senior Grand Prix event and all last season, he'd been plagued with injuries and boot problems, injuring his right ankle in December, then the left. Ten admitted that two days after he returned from Osaka, his mood was low. "I was really, really disgusted," he admitted. He was still not fully recovered from the injuries when he won that world championship silver medal three weeks later.

Ten, a true artist, according to Lori Nichol, who created his routine to "The Artist," said the Kazakhstani is incredibly sensitive to everything. Call it the Princess and the Pea syndrome. He's aware of the slightest tweak of his blade or the fit of his boot. "For athletes like that, it is extraordinarily difficult to have a decent pair of boots they feel good in," she said. "Add the boot problems to the injuries and he has never really had truly consistent training."

"I had so many rough skates, really hard times," Ten said. Coach Frank Carroll was always there for him, reminding him that the real prize was the world championship. With only three weeks to the world championship, Ten reached an aha moment, realizing that the game wasn't over. "I wanted to show everyone that I was still playing," he said. From that moment on, Ten had only one thought in his mind: doing well at the world championships. In bed, he thought of nothing else. Carroll didn't know it, but Ten worked out (doing unspecified tasks) in his garage until 10 p.m. each night. "I was on some mission," he said.

For the free skate, under a new pressure he'd never felt before, Ten decided not to think about medals, but rather to imagine that he'd already blown it. That took off the pressure, allowed him to skate with freedom, and his performance was one for the ages. Despite not having been able to sleep the two nights before the final, he won the free skate over three-time world champion Patrick Chan. Ten fell to his knees and kissed the ice.

In fact, Ten's free skate score of 174.92 was the fifth highest score of the season, only a couple of points behind Chan's best effort. And his total score of 266.48 was the fourth highest score of the year. Where had all of that come from so suddenly?

"I never thought I would finish the season this way," he said. "My free program hasn't gone well all season…I was waiting for this moment so long."

Ten didn't have world championship medals in his mind when he began to skate at an open-air rink in Almaty, Kazakhstan as a youngster. (These rinks were actually soccer fields that were transformed into ice rinks in the winter.) And yes, he really is from Kazakhstan. He's not some Russian with the right passport. Instead, he's a member of the Korean minority in Kazakhstan, and the great, great grandson of Min Keung-ho, a Korean general who fought for independence in his country. "Sometimes I think he watches me and I have no chance to fail him or disappoint him," Ten said. He feels an additional responsibility to his descendant to carry the torch.

The new attitude worked. It was as if Ten could do no wrong at the world championships. Buoyed by what he sensed was a sympathetic audience, Ten landed a quadruple toe loop, and a perfect triple Axel in the short program, inspiring a standing ovation. That put him in second place, incredibly, ahead of a couple of world champions and a European champion. His 91.56 points was the fourth highest score all season for a short program. It was his best skate in four years, he said.

"I was ready for it," he said. "When I stepped on the ice, I was really confident I would have enough strength. But it still feels like a dream that I am still sleeping in and it's time to wake up soon."

After Ten had skated for two years in the outdoor elements, Almaty got a very cold covered rink – but the temperatures dropped to minus 17 degrees Celsius inside during the winter. "I still remember how my mother would put three pairs of pants on me," he said. "I was like a cabbage.

"It helped me to be quicker," he said jokingly.

Then he moved to shopping malls, which had ice surfaces that weren't exactly Olympic-sized. Every Friday, the malls would stage an ice exhibition and Ten would perform for "all of the shopaholics," he said. He didn't feel frustrated by the meagre conditions. He didn't know anything else existed.

When he was 10, he moved to Russia to train, and learned the ropes under Elena (Vodorezova) Buianova, the first Soviet female skater to win a world championship medal (bronze in 1983) and now a master coach in Russia. "In real life, he is actually rather quiet," Buianova said. "Very quiet. Very shy. But he transforms on the ice and becomes so emotional. He jumps easily, like a cat. He has phenomenal jumping ability." Ten spent seven years there with his mother, Oksana, a violinist. (His first language is Russian). "I became a normal skater there," he said. His father, back home, was an engineer with his own business. His brother, Alexei, also stayed home. When Ten competed at the Vancouver Olympics, he was the youngest male figure skater at the Games, aged 16. He finished 11th.

When he moved to California in 2010, with his mother in tow, chief cook and manager, Ten was taken back to basics by new coach Frank Carroll. And Lori Nichol began to choreograph his routines.

"He's a good spirit," Nichol said. "He's very intelligent. He is very compassionate and caring, and when you're working on the ice and I give 150 per cent, he's giving 150 per cent back." While having his routines to "The Artist" movie soundtrack choreographed, Ten spent a month in Toronto, soaking up all the nuances he could from Nichol. Others usually spend far less time.

In trying to find the proper performance vehicle for Ten last season, Nichol had written down only one piece of music for Ten last year – "The Artist" – when usually she offers six or seven options. When Ten arrived in Toronto – before she had a chance to show him her choice – he blurted that he had seen "The Artist" on the airplane on the way to Canada. "It was so incredible? Do you know it?" he asked her. She opened her notebook and showed him her choice. "Wow, that's cool," he said.

From track to track, the music was so varied and so usable for skating, that off-handedly, Nichol suggested that they use it all, and do the first part for the short program, and the second for the long. Carroll agreed to the unusual plan.

Over the past few years, Ten has gained an immense trust of Carroll. "Whatever I have to do, just tell me and I'll do it," he tells the veteran coach.

"I had a long way from being a kid, skating like a cabbage," he said. "And now I skate in a good costume at worlds. So many things to take in. I'm glad I have this medal and I'm proud of my parents for being so patient."

From time to time, Ten gives seminars to budding young skaters back in Kazakhstan and still considers that he lives there. He says Kazakhstan now has many gorgeous rinks and there are many young skaters who want to follow his path. And Kazakhstan is quickly becoming a modern country with the wealth of oil. In 1998, its leaders decided to move the capital of the country from Almaty to the steppes where donkeys used to tread, and build a new city, Astana, from scratch. It's now the second largest city in Kazakhstan.

"Soon I believe we will have new stars," Ten said. "I feel that I am a tank, making the road for small stars."

Vera **Bazarova** &
Yuri **Larionov**
Russia

Born: Bazarova: Jan. 28, 1993; Larionov: Aug. 19, 1986

Coach: Nina Mozer

Best Results: Second at 2012 European championship, 5th at 2011 world championships

FOR THE PAST FIVE DECADES, RUSSIAN SKATERS HAVE RULED PAIR SKATING. SKATERS FROM THE SOVIET UNION OR RUSSIA HAVE WON 12 OLYMPIC GOLD MEDALS IN THE SPORT SINCE 1964 WHEN LUDMILA AND OLEG PROTOPOPOV DAZZLED THE WORLD WITH THEIR DEATH SPIRALS AND ARTISTIC STYLE OF SKATING. SINCE THE PROTOPOPOVS HAVE COMPETED, RUSSIAN or Soviet skaters have won 33 world championship titles. Russians have a way of pairing up people who can throw and twist and jump together like no other nation. Its pair skating strength came from two dominant centres of skating: Moscow and St. Petersburg.

Vera Bazarova and Yuri Larionov are a little different. They have found a completely different path to world and Olympic competition, coming from the backwaters of the country, and training for most of their careers outside of Moscow. Bazarova was born in Ekaterinaburg, the fourth largest city in Russia, but off in the Urals. Larionov was born in Novosibirsk, the third largest city in Russia, but in southwestern Siberia, where the winters are cold and long and the temperature can fall to -35 degrees Celsius on occasion. Many would find the winters in Novosibirsk tough, to say the least.

Larionov's skating career began in Tashkent, Uzbekistan (which has never been a figure skating hotbed), after his father was stationed there, working for the Russian army. Rather chubby as a child and sickly, his mother wanted to enrol him in a skating group, but his father resisted. But, as the story goes, as soon as his father left town on a business trip, Larionov's mother slipped him down to the rink and signed him up. Later, his father relented and turned into a supporter. Larionov's skating career looks like a roadmap of Russia. At one point, his family moved back to chilly Novosibirsk. Larionov also trained in Moscow for four years, but frustrated with an injury, almost retired. His coaches in Perm persuaded him to go to veteran coach Ludmila Kalinina in Perm.

A year later, Kalinina matched Bazarova and Larionov together. She had watched Bazarova arrive as a 12-year-old who knew nothing about pairs. Two years later, Bazarova and Larionov won a silver medal at the junior world championship, and during the 2007-2008 season, they began to win medals in senior Grand Prix events. In December of 2007, they won gold at the Junior Grand Prix Final.

In January, 2008, the promise of the team

that he could not look anybody in the eye after that. They had to return their gold medal from the Junior Grand Prix Final, and were not able to compete at the junior world championships. Later, with a change in doping rules, the suspension was reduced to 18 months and Larionov went back to work for the 2009-2010 season. Bazarova stood by her man, refusing to skate for others, although she had offers. By June of 2010, the team confirmed that they were in a relationship.

During their comeback year, their world opened up when they won a bronze medal at Russian nationals. Bazarova came back better than ever, and started landing triple toe loop jumps, which always escaped her as a junior. This got them onto teams for the European championships for the first time (where they were fifth), the Olympic Games in Vancouver (11th), and the world championships (eighth).

The following year, the Russian skating federation and the Ministry of Sport realized they needed to get them to better facilities than they could find in Perm, so Valinina, a coach who has a degree in chemical engineering of all things, left behind her life and all her friends and moved to Saransk in 2011, where the ice wasn't always reflooded and the acoustics weren't sophisticated. But the rink had other benefits that attracted Bazarova and Larionov: choreographic sessions with legendary Bolshoi ballerina Ludmila Vlasova, a force in the turnaround of the pair's career. "It was not very nice to listen to reproaches from the federation and read in the press that [our performance] does not cause any feeling," Bazarova said of their former efforts. At times, there was no emotional connection between the two at all on ice. And they heard plenty about their own shortcomings. But even

all came unravelled when Larionov tested positive for furosemide, a diuretic often used to mask other drugs. Larionov explained that he had taken medication for a headache, not realizing it contained a banned substance. But no explanation averted the positive test and Larionov was suspended from competition for two years. Larionov was shocked and told a reporter

in the off-season, they continued to work with Vlasova. Her presence in the room alone inspired them, she said.

But the season of 2012-13 was like a bumper-car ride for the unusual pair, he a tall burly strongman, she tiny, slender as a pencil, lacking strength. Bazarova suffers from a recurring hip injury, and it caused them to withdraw from the Nebelhorn Trophy in Germany early in the season. Fortunately, the hip did not require surgery; She deals with it through physiotherapy and massage. The problem manifests itself with weakness, not pain.

When they did get on track, they won their first gold medal at the NHK Trophy and with their second-place finish at the Rostelecom Cup in Russia, they qualified for the Grand Prix Final, where they took the silver medal. But shortly afterward, they had another setback. Larionov's boots had broken during exhibitions for the Grand Prix Final and they could not be fixed. He had to break in new boots, and according to Russian federation president Alexander Gorshkov, the difficulties of breaking in boots – which can be painful – would add to the risk element of a pair. But they also missed the European championships when Larionov injured his wrist and required surgery in Moscow.

Shortly afterward, they decided to leave Kalinina, after eight years together, saying they knew they needed a push to improve further. While preparing for the world championships, they used elderly master coach Victor Kudriavtsev as a stop-gap measure. He's known as a coach of singles skaters such as Sergei Volkov, the first Soviet man to win a world title, and 1998 Olympic champion Ilia Kulik. But he was also known as the coach of a high-level pair team Ludmila Smirnova and Andrei Suraykin, who won an Olympic silver medal in 1972. Kudriavtsev was only a temporary arrangement. At 75, he's basically retired, although he now works as a consultant for the Russian federation.

With all of the scrambling, it was no surprise that the 2013 world championship performances of Bazarova and Larionov were not up to their potential. Bazarova singled her triple toe loop in the short program, which placed them in seventh. She was devastated. "I never do that," she said. "I always go for it." Larionov figured that their lack of competition hurt them.

Bazarova did land her triple toe loop in the long program, although not in unison with her partner, and they made errors on another jump. The rest of their elements were done well, but not executed with excellence, and they finished seventh overall, lowest of the three Russian teams. The 1984 Olympic pair champion from Russia, Oleg Vasiliev, at the world championships as a coach for another team, said he was not thrilled with the performance of Bazarova and Larionov. Still, he recognized that they'd had a tough season with changes in coach, changing training centres and injuries. "They made stupid mistakes on the jump," Vasiliev said. "But my biggest respect for them. They came over here, they skated probably 60 to 70 percent from the maximum that they can."

But Bazarova and Larionov are not standing still. Shortly after the world championships, they announced that they would train with the reigning world champions Tatiana Volosozhar and Maxim Trankov under Nina Mozer, whose first task was to help Bazarova get completely healthy. Both teams will help each other.

Caydee **Denney** & John **Coughlin**
United States

Born: Denney: June 22, 1993; Coughlin: Dec. 1, 1985

Coach: Dalilah Dappenfield

Best results: 8th at 2012 world championships, second at 2012 Four Continents, won 2012 U.S. championships

*I*N THE UNITED STATES, PAIR SKATERS RIDE A WILD MERRY-GO-ROUND, CHANGING PARTNERS AND SEARCHING FOR ANSWERS IN THEIR PURSUIT OF OLYMPIC GLORY. EVEN A LITTLE WORLD CHAMPIONSHIP GLORY WOULD HELP. AMERICAN PAIR SKATERS HAVE NEVER WON AN OLYMPIC TITLE, ALTHOUGH 1979 WORLD CHAMPIONS TAI BABILONIA AND RANDY GARDNER WERE TABBED as favorites for Olympic gold on their home turf at Lake Placid, N.Y. in 1980. But at the eleventh hour, they were forced to withdraw, Gardner hobbled by a groin injury. The withdrawal haunted them for years. The Olympics has not been kind to American pair skaters since.

The last Olympic pair medal won by an American team was in 1988 at the Calgary Games when Jill Watson and Peter Oppegard earned bronze, 26 years before Sochi. The Americans haven't won a gold medal at the world championships since Babilonia and Gardner in 1979, and the most recent medalists of any colour were from Kyoko Ina and John Zimmerman, bronze medalists at the 2002 world championships in Nagano.

The journey to these Olympics in Sochi has been particularly trying for U.S. pair skaters. Few of the aspirants have been together very long. The last five U.S. pair championships have been won by five different teams, many of them no longer together. But Caydee Denney and a battered and bruised John Coughlin, in their third season together, will try to catch the leading contenders from the dominant countries: Russia, Germany and Canada and now to a lesser extent, China.

Unlike Babilonia and Gardner, Denney and Coughlin didn't even make it to the world championships that precede an Olympics. Nor did they make it to the 2013 U.S. championships, leaving Alexa Scimeca and Chris Knierim as the favourites to win, even though they had been together only eight months. Sure enough, somebody else won the U.S. title: Marissa Castelli and Simon Schnapir, who perhaps benefitted from the fact that they had been skating together for almost seven years and had a history: a bronze medal at the world junior championships.

Coughlin had five previous partners before Denney, including Caitlin Yankowskas, with whom he won the 2011 U.S. title. Denney had an on-again, off-again partnership with Jeremy Barrett, with whom she won the 2010 U.S. championship. Coughlin had just finished sixth at the 2011 world championship with Yankowskas and just

as it looked as if they were set to climb the world ladder, the partnership dissolved and Coughlin, the son of a retired police officer, figured it might be best to retire. He just wasn't happy, he said. He'd come off a season that drained him. He failed to make the Olympic team in Vancouver and his mother, Stacy, died in February 2010. His free skate to "Ave Maria" that season, dedicated to his mother, was inspiring.

Denney had skated at the 2010 Olympics with Barrett and finished 13th, but their partnership ended when her blade sliced his right calf during a practice session. The injury required 41 stitches.

Denney's mother, Deedee, engineered a tryout with Coughlin, and instantly they knew they had a future. So powerful was Coughlin, that the first time they tried a triple twist, Denney felt that she actually rotated 3 ½ times. Denney moved from Florida to train with Coughlin at Colorado Springs.

They seemed an unlikely pair, but actually, they are perfect for pair skating. Denney stands 14 inches shorter than Coughlin, a behemoth at 6-foot-2. And Denney is eight years younger. Together, they are an athletic pair, with explosive, enormous triple twists, done with ease. At their first world championship together in 2012, they executed a difficult and long lift at the very end of their long program. Coughlin looked tireless.

Denney was a jade-coloured gem, matching his every long stroke.

Their goal is lofty: standing on the podium at a world championship or an Olympics. They are well aware of the gloomy U.S. statistics at such events for pair skaters. But just to make their lives more interesting, Coughlin developed pain in his left hip during the fall of 2012. The question? Continue on to the U.S. championships? Or withdraw, miss the world championships – an Olympic qualifier – and get surgery to repair the torn labrum? On Dec. 4, 2012, Coughlin underwent surgery. He was off the ice for nine weeks, but they were back in full training by April.

Back on track, the team is taking a new direction: having Canadian choreographer Julie Marcotte design both their short and long programs for the Olympic season, taking a page from Castelli and Schnapir, who used a Marcotte routine to win their U.S. title in 2013. Marcotte designs programs for Canadian champions Meagan Duhamel and Eric Radford, bronze medalists at the 2013 world championships.

Their Olympic programs? Their short program is to music from the animated movie "Anastasia," a tip of the hat to the site of the Olympics in Russia. The free? Something meant to bring goosebumps: "Casablanca." They are determined. And hopeful.

Meagan **Duhamel** & Eric **Radford**
Canada

Born: Duhamel: Dec. 8, 1985; Radford: Jan. 27, 1985

Coaches: Richard Gauthier, Bruno Marcotte, Sylvie Fullum

Best Results: third at the 2013 world championships, won the 2013 Four Continents championships, second at the 2013 World Team Trophy

THERE WILL BE NO SLEEPING BEAUTY BALLETS, NO CHOPIN ETUDES, NO HAUNTING BOLEROS, NOR EVEN ANY LOVE STORIES FOR WORLD BRONZE PAIR MEDALISTS MEAGAN DUHAMEL AND ERIC RADFORD ON THEIR TREK TO THE SOCHI OLYMPIC GAMES. THEY ARE FORGING THEIR OWN PATH IN THE MUSICAL REALM.

They are an uncommon pair, he long-limbed with classical lines, she peppy, tiny, muscular and athletic. The disparity in heights helps them with twists and lifts, not so much for throws or for matching lines. They are friends, and since they teamed up in the spring of 2010, they've become better friends. A love song wouldn't work for them. It just wouldn't ring true. But the silliness of "Alice in Wonderland" has never been used by pair skaters. And this also matters: When choreographer Julie Marcotte first heard the highlights and the lowlights of the music, images of moves instantly danced in her head. That's always a good sign.

But it's the short program music that will stop hearts. Called "Tribute," it is composed by Radford himself, who has been playing the piano as long as he's been skating, from age eight. "I would say that music is just as important a part of my life as skating," he said. Music composition is in his future when skating's bright lights fade. He studied music for two years at York University before he moved to Montreal to skate.

And he's working on gaining his Grade 10 at the Royal Conservatory of Music. When he moved to Montreal, he continued to study piano, until his teacher moved away.

That puts Radford in a rare category in this sport. He's not only an artist on the ice, he's an artist in the studio, composing and creating his own music. Most skaters just don't do these things, unless your name is Dmitri Dmitrenko, who won the world junior championships in 1992 in Hull, Que., for the Soviet Union and finally, as a skater for Ukraine, gold and bronze medals at European championships. As Dmitrenko grew up, so did his unconventional side and he did some of his own choreography, too. He would create synthesized music in a Kiev studio with a couple of friends and came up with concepts like "I Did," or video games (once skating with a CD glued to his back.) In 1994, his fertile imagination came up with music he called "The Fly." After a choreographer talked him out of emoting the life of a fly, he inserted a move in which he slapped his hands together, to kill the insect, of course.

He liked to write his own music because he said he could feel it and understand it better. He did not want to look like another skater. His wonky themes prevented that.

But Radford's theme and work is indeed serious and very professional. He wrote the song for piano two days after his coach of six years, Paul Wirtz, died of non-Hodgkin's lymphoma in 2006. Stirred by the tragedy, Radford still remembers the exact date of the death of a coach who had guided him since he was 15. "It was the most formative years of my life," Radford said. "That's why he had such a huge impact on me. I really feel like he made me into the skater that I am. He gave me my jumps. He kind of molded me into being a classical kind of skater. And he taught me how to compete." Radford wrote the music as a tribute to Wirtz. It just came to him.

Radford originally wrote a version that he wanted to use for himself as a singles skater. But when he moved to Germany years ago to train with Ingo Steuer, the former world champion told Radford to forget about the singles discipline to avoid injury and focus only on pairs.

The music-composing plan went onto the shelf until August of 2012, when Radford could see a future at the Olympics, after having been paired with Duhamel. (Steuer had once considered pairing him with Tatiana Volosozhar.) He turned his Tribute into an orchestral version, using a computer program that allows him to drop the sounds of other musical instruments on top of a piano recording. When Marcotte heard it for the first time, she really didn't think it was very good. "He had an agreement with Julie that if in the end, the music was not good enough, that we are not going to use it," said coach Richard Gauthier. At first, Duhamel was worried about the music, too. The short program is vital. So many things can go wrong that can take a pair out of contention before the long program.

Radford was undeterred. "If I was going to use it for Olympic year, I wanted to do it right," he said. So he googled "music composer Montreal" and clicked on the first website he saw: Louis Babin. Babin himself answered the phone when the skater called. Babin was intrigued by Radford's idea to turn the piece into an Olympic competitive routine.

On April 2, 2013, after the world championships, Radford hired a 16-piece string orchestra to play his piece at a Montreal studio with the help of Babin and a new version of his composition

was born. Other instruments were to be inserted digitally. At last, almost exactly seven years after Radford had initially composed the score, there it was, before him, notes and sounds that had been in his heart for so long, filling the room. "It felt like electricity going through my body," he said. "The feeling was comparable to standing on the podium at worlds. It was like hearing a part of you come alive." Tears welled up in his eyes. Gauthier thought it "was pretty good." Marcotte played a vital role in the final version of the music. She suggested where the musical highlights should be.

When they use the music during the season, it may well be a tribute to Wirtz for Radford, deep in his heart, but Duhamel has to relate to it as well. Together, they will be skating a tribute to all of the people who helped them get to Olympic year.

And it almost didn't happen for either of them. Neither qualified for the Vancouver Olympics, while skating with other partners. Duhamel and Craig Buntin finished third at the Canadian championships that preceded the Olympics, but Canada had only two Olympic berths for pair skaters.

After the Vancouver Olympics, Duhamel thought she was finished with figure skating. She'd had enough. She'd had suffered from a stress fracture, a bulging disk in her back and – for a year and a half – nerve damage in a leg. Add to that the stress of just trying to qualify for an Olympics, and Duhamel wasn't sure she wanted to put herself through that again. "I didn't even know if I'd make it to the end of the season, let alone dedicate myself to another four years of skating," she said at the time. "It was a low point in my life."

She took eight weeks away from skating after

her final competition of the year, and felt the pain of her injuries melt away. At her lowest point, she realized all she wanted to do was skate again. She was 24, not young for a pair skater starting all over again, but yet not as old as China's Shen Xue and Zhao Hongbo, who were 31 and 36 respectively when they won the Vancouver Olympics.

The last person she thought she'd ever team up with was Radford, who had also fallen short of fulfillment as a pair skater; Their differences made the union seemed unlikely. But both are from small-town Northern Ontario: Duhamel from Lively, Ont., where both of her parents worked two jobs to keep her in skating; Radford from Balmertown, as far north as you can go by road in Ontario. "Balmertown makes Lively look like New York," Duhamel joked.

If Duhamel and Radford were skeptical about their future on the first day of a tryout, Gauthier, who had matched Jamie Sale with David Pelletier, urged them to give it a week, to be patient. Sure enough, they gelled within that week. In fact, they complemented each other, "filled each other's holes," as Duhamel put it. Their greatest asset is their friendship.

"The one thing they had, was they both had the same goals," Gauthier said. "They wanted it together and skating was their priority. The coaches at the club in St. Leonard, Que., gave the pair all of the right tools, but Duhamel and Radford do more, on their own initiative. Last season, they took acting lessons to improve their presentation mark. All last season, they had the highest technical marks in the world, thanks to their side-by-side triple Lutzes – by far the most difficult jump of any of the elite teams. The Lutzes are their aces. Both are strong jumpers, aided by their singles careers.

And they do a rare throw triple Lutz, both

in the short and long program. Last season, the Canadian team also did a three-jump combination in the second half of their long program routine, when the mark increases by 10 per cent. It didn't come by magic. Every morning at St. Leonard, Duhamel and Radford were the first skaters onto the ice for practice and the last ones to leave.

This time the Sochi Olympics will come along at the right time for Duhamel and Radford in a sport where timing is important. "It takes three years to build a team," Gauthier said. Sale and Pelletier won a world championship three years after they joined forces and an Olympic gold medal in their fourth year. All last year, Duhamel and Radford were determined to win a world championship medal, a bronze, after being fifth the previous year. They exceeded their expectations, finishing second in the short program ahead of four-time world champions Aliona Savchenko and Robin Szolkowy of Germany for the first time in their careers. It seemed surreal to Radford, who had trained with them in Germany for a time. The long program was another story. Radford struggled to put up a lift, but succeeded: the Germans backpedaled on both of their jumping passes, the spins lost unison slightly, and although she landed an ambitious throw triple Axel, it was on two feet. When the German's marks came up, placing them ahead of Duhamel and Radford, the large crowd booed and whistled in protest. "Our skating was not as good as our points," Szolkowy had said after the short. Duhamel and Radford weren't complaining. "This is like gold to us," they said of their bronze.

But winning that bronze medal is an important step for the Canadian team enroute to Sochi. "We're not just participating in the Olympics

anymore," Radford said. "We wanted to set ourselves up to be contenders in Sochi." Even though Duhamel will be 28 years old by the time of the Sochi Games, and Radford will be 29, Gauthier believes they will continue for the next quadrennial. By then, the Germans, the Russians and the Chinese will be gone, out of the way, and therefore so will all the roadblocks to the top. That is, unless they take the roadblocks out themselves. During Olympic season, Gauthier says, judges may be more willing to give them high marks. After all, they're world medalists, now.

Kirsten **Moore-Towers** & Dylan **Moscovitch**
Canada

Born: Moore-Towers: July 1, 1992; Moscovitch: Sept. 23, 1984

Coaches: Kristy and Kris Wirtz

Best results: fourth at the 2013 world championships, second at the 2013 Four Continents championships, 2011 Canadian champions

TODDLERS THEY WERE, BUT NO LESS IMMUNE TO THE LURE OF THE OLYMPIC GAMES, FOR ALL OF THEIR INNOCENCE.

DYLAN MOSCOVITCH'S PARENTS TOOK HIM SKATING ONE DAY WHEN HE WAS 13 MONTHS OLD, BUNDLED IN A BABY BACKPACK. NOT ALLOWED TO TAKE HIM ONTO THE ICE IN SUCH FASHION, THEY RENTED SOME TINY DOUBLE BLADED SKATES

for him. Cheese cutters, he calls them now. And off little Moscovitch went, bopping across the ice like a young robin finding its wings. A career was born.

"After that, I just wanted to skate all the time," he said.

When Moscovitch was five years old, someone asked him if he wanted to go to the Olympics. "No," he replied. "I want to win the Olympics."

Kirsten Moore-Towers' mother (an adult synchronized skater, for fun) took her skating one day in St. Catharines, Ont. and the tiny girl had the opposite reaction to the slippery surface. "I absolutely hated it," she said. "I never wanted to go on the ice again."

Her mother, Sherry, director of finance for a retirement home, insisted that as soon as Kirsten learned how to skate, she could quit. She just had to finish out her lessons. By the time she had come to the end of the lessons, she was hooked. Before long, little blond Kirsten was bombing around the ice, probably only three or four years old, and hugging her friends every time she

whipped by. "I think I've always been peppy," she admitted.

She was only five when she saw Tara Lipinski win a gold medal at the 1998 Olympic Games, and the dream took root. And the urge grew after she watched her favourite skater, Sarah Hughes, win the Olympics in Salt Lake City four years later. Hughes hadn't been the favourite to win. She had upset the cart. Anything seemed possible to Moore-Towers after that.

Moore-Towers wasn't allowed to stay up and watch the women's event at Salt Lake City because the two-hour time difference put the event past her bedtime. But her mother woke her up early the next morning and she watched the whole event before school. "I was thrilled," she said. "And really motivated from then on."

But not as a pair skater. Moore-Towers turned down all offers to skate pairs when she was younger, intent to follow the paths of two young Olympian single skaters. By age 14, she was landing triple Lutzes. She finished sixth at the junior women's level at the 2008 Canadian championships.

Meanwhile, Moscovitch, the oldest of four children, filled up his days with all sorts of sports pursuits. Name it, he did it: hockey, dodge ball, baseball, basketball, volleyball, karate . But figure skating took over. Is it any surprise that he juggled pair and single skating, at times competing against his best friends, Eric Radford and Bryce Davison, who also competed in both disciplines? But Moscovitch made his name first as a pair skater, teamed up with his youngest sister, Kyra, who was nine years younger.

When they joined forces, Kyra was only nine years old. They won the national pre-novice championship when she was only 10 – and he was 19.

When they first teamed up, Kyra was only 4-foot-9, but as the years passed, she grew to 5-foot-6, tall for a female pair skater. But their biggest roadblock was the age difference between them. For years, Kyra was too young to compete in senior international events, and Dylan too old to compete in junior, frustrating because of their talent. Kyra was landing all of her triples by the time she was 12.

They moved away from home to train in Waterloo, Ont., and Dylan was put in the role of parent, in charge of a girl pushing into her teens. It was as dramatic as it sounded. They lived together in an apartment building, and then Moore-Towers moved in down the hall. Kyra and Kirsten hit it off: they were best friends. By this time, Moore-Towers had been talked into skating pairs with Andrew Evans, with whom she had a budding career.

But just as the Moscovitches were about to take flight and get international competitions, Kyra developed scoliosis of the spine, which made it too painful for her to continue skating. She retired and is now a student at McGill

University. And Moore-Towers and Evans split up, too, after 10 months together.

It wasn't a stretch for coach Kris Wirtz to match Moore-Towers with Moscovitch in the spring of 2009. Their career immediately took off when Jessica Dube and Bryce Davison had to withdraw from Skate Canada in Kingston, Ont., because of Davison's career-ending injury. Moscovitch visited Davison in the hospital on the way to the event and then he and Moore-Towers won a silver medal. Because they also won a silver medal at Skate America, they qualified for the Grand Prix Final, an event reserved for the top six teams, a remarkable effort for their first season together. They had gone from zero to 60 in less than a year.

"I remember being nervous," Moore-Towers said. "I have always been a bit of a stress case. I'm a lot better now, but when we started, Dylan took on the role of calming me down and making sure I was always comfortable in my surroundings."

Now the pair has gelled and can be considered among the best in the world, with their extremely difficult lifts (for example, Moscovitch lifting his partner from a kneeling position on the ice) solid throws and twists, their speed and their ability to excite. They won the free skate at the 2013 Four Continents Championships over friends and archrivals Meagan Duhamel and Eric Radford, and many thought they should have been on the podium at the world championships. (They were fourth, after scoring the second highest technical mark in the free skate.)

They are on a perfect trajectory for Sochi, this striking pair with disparate outlooks. Moscovitch looks outward, always, and is a certified Krav Maga instructor; It's an Israeli military combat system that is more akin to self-defence. "It's funny," Moscovitch said. "I'm not at all a violent person. I was raised not being allowed to even have water guns. My mom is very anti-violence. But I have always had a fascination with martial arts, and fighting arts."

For four years, he learned at the feet of kungfu sifu (master) Glen Doyle, who also worked with Elvis Stojko. The martial arts teach focus, an asset for a figure skater fighting for an Olympic medal.

And Moore-Towers, nestled at night with her tiny Shortie dog (one quarter Shitzu and three-quarters Yorkie), says figure skating is it for her. "Nothing ever drove me like figure skating did," she said. "I still like it. I don't love it every day. I think if anybody tells you that, they are probably lying. There are harder days than others.

"But I'm excited to be here. If I take a week off, I miss it by the end. I'm always excited to get new programs and try new things. Heaven forbid that I would ever be forced to quit because I don't know what I would do."

That from the kid who once wanted nothing to do with a slippery ice surface.

Pang Qing & Tong Jian

China

Born: Pang: Dec. 24, 1979; Tong: Aug. 15, 1979

Coach: Yao Bin

Best Results: two-time world champions, second at the 2010 Olympics

EVERYTHING HURTS, EXCEPT THEIR LOVE.

OFTEN FORGOTTEN, OFTEN UNDERRATED, OFTEN BESIEGED BY INJURY, AT LEAST IN RECENT YEARS, PANG QING AND TONG JIAN ARE SOLDIERING ON TO THE SOCHI OLYMPICS, WITH WHAT'S LEFT OF THEIR KNEES AND LOFTY AMBITIONS. AT LEAST THEY HOPE THEY WILL MAKE IT. IF THEY DO, IT WILL BE THEIR

fourth Olympic Games. And afterwards? They will be married and life will somehow go on.

Always in the shadows of 2010 Olympic champions Shen Xue and Zhao Hongbo, Pang and Tong have struggled for respect from the beginning. Does anybody remember that Pang and Tong won the free skate at the Vancouver Olympics and set a world record of 141.81 points for that portion of the event? "I kissed the ice at the end of the program," Tong said. "I don't know what got into me. I felt this power that made me do it."

They took the Olympic silver medal and then won the 2010 world championships in Turin, Italy, a month later, without Shen and Zhao in the mix. And no wonder the Olympic moment was memorable for this couple who skated to The Impossible Dream that season. They had accomplished the impossible by doing what they did.

And now they are set to try again. After finishing fifth (sixth in the short, fourth in the long) at the 2013 world championships, their 14th consecutive one), Tong said sadly that his first mission

when he returned to China was to get to a hospital to check out his troublesome knees. "We need to figure out the pain," he said. He does not know why they hurt, but they give him anguish when he flexes his knees. It's okay to walk. To land triple toe loops? Not so much. Pang has also been suffering from knee problems, too.

Last season was a difficult one for the two-time world champions (2006 and 2010), because for so many years, they had no troubles like this. The previous season, they competed only once, at the 2012 world championships in Nice, France. "But knees for a skater is very important," Tong said.

How are they going to get to Sochi? "Do you remember that our 2010 long program was the Impossible Dream?" said Tong. "So will Sochi be. We know it will be hard, but I hope we keep good skating."

Their mistakes were minor in the short program in London. Tong stumbled out of a two-foot landing on a triple toe loop. Pang lost her footing at the end of a step sequence. It was enough to place them sixth. They had taken

a month off after Grand Prix Final in Sochi to allow him to recover. They finished a fraction of a point behind Canadians Meagan Duhamel and Eric Radford in the free skate, skating on grit and will for their best long program of the season.

Over the years, many have written them off, and Pang and Tong have been caught between two dynasties. Shen and Zhao were stars on anybody's radar and the athletic Zhang Dan and Zhang Hao won an Olympic silver medal in Turin, after improving very quickly. Pang and Tong were left to pick up all the pieces they left.

Pang and Tong (and Shen and Zhao) were born in the gritty industrial city of Harbin, known for its winter ice sculptures and frosty rinks. When Shen and Zhao headed off to Beijing for training with coach Yao Bin, Pang and Tong were left behind to train on their own because the Chinese federation just didn't have the resources to take both teams.

Pang and Tong waited wistfully in the cold back home, thinking that they'd be called to Beijing in a day or two, according to a Chinese news agency. They waited months, then years. By the third year, they got the green light, and two days after they arrived at the Capital Athletic Centre in Bejiing, Pang broke a bone in a fall from a throw. They had to return home to Harbin. And there they stayed for another two years.

During these dismal days, Pang and Tong fought and argued. Sometimes they'd just pack up and go home and stop training. Both were stubborn. They needed a coach to settle the differences.

At this time, Tong had a chance of becoming a professional dancer in a provincial dance company according to the story in a Chinese publication. If he had decided to take this route, his skating career would have ended. As it happened,

he did spend two years as an ice dancer, and this relatively brief sideline always lived on in his exquisite line and power of expression. In the beginning, Tong was the star of the pair. In later years, the fragile-looking Pang caught up to him.

Facing two choices, waiting for the call to Beijing, or deciding to quit skating, Pang and Tong placed their faith in Yao. And waited. Their parents weren't happy about this state of limbo. They would have preferred them to continue studying.

But in 1997, when they finally got the call to Beijing, Pang and Tong always had catching up to do. During the early years, Pang and Tong were handed down Shen and Zhao's used skates, costumes, choreography, everything. "Any guarantee of training was also given to them," Tong told the Chinese newspaper. "Later on, that we could compete with them at all was already a big revolution."

Pang and Tong had considered taking a break after the Vancouver Olympic season, but with Shen and Zhao retired, the team decided to stay in the game to earn placements for the Chinese.

With Shen and Zhao gone, Pang and Tong still had to outskate the Zhangs (who are not related.) The Zhangs, paired together the same year that Pang and Tong finally arrived in Beijing, were precocious, exciting youngsters, who were sent out on the Junior Grand Prix circuit (Pang and Tong had no junior international career), and won the junior world championship and other events with deadly arsenals like quadruple twists.

The Zhangs had their own skates, their own costumes and their own choreography, which helped their meteoric rise. Pang and Tong could never expect those things for themselves.

Pang and Tong may have been older than the Zhangs, but the Chinese No. 2 team had lost five

him to do twists (big high lofty, flying twists, for which the Chinese are legendary.). Deciding to take the time to perfect the quality of their routines, and craft their new routines, they skipped much of the 2011-2012 season and did only the world championships, at which they finished fourth. It was a year in which they wanted to stretch themselves, and present more popular music. After so many world championships, they wanted to evolve. They had been medal contenders for 11 of those world championships. If they make it to Sochi, it will be their fourth Olympic Games, rare in the figure skating world. They will both be 34 years old.

Nor are they giving up anything for Sochi. In their plans, they've talked about preparing quad throws or quad twists for Sochi, but all of it is still under discussion. Wonky knees may have a say in that.

And then, there's always life after Sochi for this pair that tugs at the heartstrings. For years, Tong stated that they had never dated, that it was impossible to maintain a proper working relationship with entanglements of the heart. But at the conclusion of the Arts on Ice skating show in Shanghai in June of 2011, Tong dropped to one knee on centre ice, gathered a bouquet of flowers in his arm and proposed marriage to Pang.

"I didn't expect this until I saw the roses," Pang said. "My mind went blank at that moment, but after that, I was extremely happy. Thanks Tong. You have given me a wonderful proposal."

"Before the Vancouver Winter Games, claiming an Olympic medal was my dream, but now my dream is to have you with me forever," Tong said to Pang, driven to happy tears.

Tong helped design Pang's ring, which is carved with a snowflake, an endearing symbol for them.

years of development and really were almost on a par with the younger pair that had quickly zoomed up the competitive ladder.

The willowy Pang eventually developed kidney problems, and her health is constantly being monitored. As he got older, Tong's knees began to give out, also making it difficult for

Peng Cheng & Zhang Hao, Sui Wenjing & Han Cong
China

Born: Peng: April 23, 1997; Zhang: July 6, 1984

Coach: Yao Bin

Best Results: 11th at 2013 world championships, fifth at 2013 Four Continents Championship

Born: Sui: July 18, 1995; Han: Aug. 6, 1992

Coach: Luan Bo

Best results: three-time world junior champions, 2012 Four Continents champions

COACH YAO BIN HAS SINGLEHANDEDLY CREATED A POWERHOUSE OF PAIR SKATERS IN CHINA FROM THIN AIR OVER THE PAST TWO DECADES. HE'S CHINA'S PREMIER SKATING COACH, A REMARKABLE MAN WITH A PHOTOGRAPHIC MEMORY, AN ABIDING KNOWLEDGE OF CLASSICAL MUSIC AND A VERSATILE MASTER OF ALL TRADES. HE'S A CONCERT PIANIST, WITH A LOVE OF FRANZ LISZT

and Peter Tchaikovsky, and has a piano in each house, one in Beijing, another in his home in his native Harbin. He's played four times for television shows in China. In the early days, he designed the costumes for his skaters.

At the Vancouver Olympics, his legendary pair skaters, Shen Xue and Zhao Hongbo, won an Olympic medal against all odds, coming back from injury. They were supposedly past their prime at ages 30 and 36. At the Games, his other team, Pang Qing and Tong Jian, won the silver medal with a world-record free skate, in which they actually defeated Shen and Zhao. Yet another team, Zhang Dan and Zhang Hao won an Olympic silver medal in 2006 in Turin.

In short, Yao's students finished second, third and fifth at the 2004 world championships in Dortmund, in the city where Yao himself made his international debut, finishing last with partner Luan Bo. At the 2010 Olympics in Vancouver, Yao's pupils were first, second and fifth.

Since 1999 when Shen and Zhao won the first Chinese world championship medal in pair

skating, the Chinese have been a factor in the race for medals in the sport's riskiest discipline. But the Sochi Olympics may prove to be a different story. Shen and Zhao have retired, and China's No. 2 team (now No. 1), Pang and Tong, is troubled by a spate of injuries. They will be 34 years old by the time of the Games in Russia. Indeed, of the six senior teams skating in China, the top three teams are all battling injuries.

"I know some fans say Chinese figure skating is declining," said Tong. "It is kind of true. We are not at our peak in terms on physical conditions and skills. The pairs in other countries.... are rising quickly. But as the whole team is facing a difficult time, we have to take the responsibility to help maintain the glory of Chinese skating." At the 2013 world figure skating championships, the Chinese clearly struggled. Pang and Tong rallied to finish fifth, while the new team of Peng Cheng and Zhang Hao finished 11th.

The aspiring young three-time world junior champions Sui Wenjing and Han Cong finished 12th of 16. This is a team with star potential, as

Sui Wenjiang and Han Cong

Peng Cheng and Zhang Hao

long as Sui doesn't outgrow Han. They teamed up together in 2007, without either of them having pair experience, inspired by Shen and Zhao. Sui and Han have landed throw quadruple Salchows and quadruple twists in competition. And they hope these will be ready for Sochi, too. Yao's old pairs partner, Luan, coaches this team.

Last season, Sui and Hong missed two months of training and basically the entire season because Sui, listed as being 17 years old, was suffering from epiphysitis in her right foot, an overuse injury that inflicts young athletes who stress their growth plates with repetitive activity. The injury can be extremely uncomfortable and may lead to retarded growth of the bone and eventually disability if left untreated, according to the Cincinnati Sports Medicine Research Foundation in Ohio. The treatment? Rest. Stop all running. Sui and Hong were forced to stay off the ice. They made their season's debut at the 2013 world championships. They didn't perform badly, but lost all chance when Sui fell on a triple toe loop that she underrotated. That put them 11th from the get-go, in the short program.

"I have been walking and skating only for two months, and so we didn't have much time to prepare and practice," Sui said. "I am very happy just to be here." Sui was nervous, understandably. "This competition was a challenge," said Han, who speaks English. "Her injury takes a long time to recover." In the long program, she underrotated both of the jumps in her program, falling once. After she finished, she coughed often.

The 2013 world championship was a challenge for Zhang, too, who had won an Olympic silver medal in Turin with Zhang Dan, who he affectionately called Dandan. Zhang Hao was left looking for a new partner when Dandan retired to attend university in China, as the tallest woman in pair skating at 5-foot-7. He teamed up with Peng Cheng, who was listed as 15 by the time of the 2013 world championships, but she arrived at the event, feeling nervous at her first world championship. She had competed pairs for only a year and Yao said he had matched her with the experienced Zhang because of her "stature and abilities." Peng had competed at only two national championships before joining forces with the massive, gregarious Zhang.

In the past year, these two Chinese pair teams have come under scrutiny for an apparent discrepancy in ages between the International Skating Union biographies and information on the

Chinese federation websites. Ages listed on the Chinese website would have made Zhang Dan too young to compete at the 2002 Olympics and world championships. They were 11th in Salt Lake City and ninth at worlds that year.

Zhang Hao's listed birthdate on the Chinese website would have made him too old to compete at the 2003 world junior championships, which he won with Zhang.

Sui and Han's ages also appeared to suggest an age discrepancy. According to the Chinese federation website, Sui would have been too young to have competed at a world junior championship that they won. They won three.

Later the ISU ruled that there were no discrepancies in the birthdates of their passports and ISU registration papers.

The ISU requires skaters to be 15 by the preceding July 1 to compete at an Olympics or senior world championships and 14 for other senior-level international competitions like Grand Prix. Junior skaters must be at least 13 the previous July 1, but cannot have turned 19 (in singles events) or 21 (for pairs and ice dancers.)

For now, the Chinese are trying to gather their forces on the international stage. Together, Peng and Zhang have already been performing quad twists in competition, but Zhang says their problem is not technical. Rather it's that they need to skate as a unit, which time and experience will solve.

But the rigours of pair skating are also affecting Zhang as much as Tong. Zhang noted that he has many problems now: in his shoulders, his back and his knees. At the 2013 Four Continents championship in Osaka, Peng showed up for a practice by herself: Zhang, hurting everywhere, and coach Yao Bin, who has long had an ailing back, too, had skipped it. Olympic victory for the Chinese this time may well be an impossible dream.

Aliona **Savchenko** & Robin **Szolkowy**
Germany

Born: Savchenko: June 19, 1984; Szolkowy: July 14, 1979

Coach: Ingo Steuer

Best Results: four-time world champions, third at the 2010 Olympics

Sure, Aliona Savchenko and Robin Szolkowy won a bronze medal at the Vancouver Olympics, but their body language during the moments following the event said something other than joy: They were downcast, clearly upset.

After a quiet chat with coach Ingo Steuer the very next morning, they decided to turn disappointment into a second chance – at the Sochi Olympics, four years away. It was a courageous decision. By the time they make it to Sochi, Savchenko will be 30 years old, Szolkowy 34. Aging pair skaters must be careful. The years of pounding and lifting and landing difficult tricks take their toll on the body. Even now, they admit that they'll try difficult moves much less during training than their younger peers. And now that they have won four world championship titles (2008, 2009, 2011, 2012), they don't feel compelled to add more. Losing one won't affect their equilibrium. Every step they take is aimed at only one goal: to get to the Sochi Olympics in fine fettle, better than anyone else and go for gold.

However, they've encountered an obstacle that wasn't there when they started down this difficult road: a new Russian team of Tatiana Volosozhar and Maxim Trankov, who won the 2013 world title by more than 20 points. But they also know that pairs skating, the riskiest of all disciplines, is unpredictable, a capricious endeavour. Anything can happen.

With one year to go to the Olympics, how far had they come? Rumblings of controversy followed their scores at the 2013 world championships. When they earned 132.09 points for their free skate, in which they had made many errors, the crowd booed and whistled the judges.

"Hey, come on," said a Eurosport commentator. "It is awful. It's awful, I'm afraid," referring to the high mark. The score put them ahead of Canadians Meagan Duhamel and Eric Radford, who had defeated them in the short program. What saved the Germans was their ambitious plan, decided after the warmup: to insert a throw triple Axel (base mark 8.25 points) at the very end of their routine, instead of a throw triple Salchow (base mark 4.95 points.) And to do such a rare and difficult element at the end of a 4 ½ minute routine, when every muscle fibre is burning? Unthinkable. Definitely dauntless and dangerous. Savchenko almost did it, landing slightly on two feet, saving 7.39 points for the plucky effort.

Savchenko and Szolkowy aren't the first skaters to land the throw triple Axel (Rena Inoue

and John Baldwin did it at home at the 2006 U.S. championships and then became the first to land it at an international event when they did it at the 2006 Olympics. The last time they landed it was at the 2010 U.S. championships. They are now retired.)

Savchenko and Szolkowy bravely took up the new element late in their careers, during the 2011-2012 season with the idea that they could perfect it by Sochi if they started the process well in advance. They had already flirted with the throw quad flip the previous season, because their throw triple flip has always been a powerful, solid element for them. But they had never used the quad, and won every event they entered that season without it.

The Germans tried the throw triple Axel first at the 2010 Skate America event, but Savchenko took a hard fall. Still the team got credit in the marks for completing the rotations. Savchenko took another hard fall in an attempt at the NHK Trophy in Japan and then they set the risky move aside until they landed it at the 2012 world championships in Nice, France. However, Savchenko's free foot lightly brushed the ice. Some judges gave them full credit for the move; Others noticed the error. They used this move to win their fourth world title, but by only .11 points over the Russians. Clearly, the element won the event for them.

At the 2013 world championships, Savchenko and Szolkowy made lots of mistakes: she doubled both parts of a triple toe loop – triple toe loop combination and then doubled a triple Salchow. He fell on that Salchow. Still, their unison on elements was impeccable, their routines always innovative (Flamenco Bolero for the long), their technique strong. They lost perhaps about 12 points on missed elements, but their program

component scores remained higher than anyone else but the Russians. Notably, Savchenko and Szolkowy scored the first perfect mark of 10 (for program components) ever given a skater in the current code-of-points judging system several years ago.

If Savchenko and Szolkowy's silver medal at the world championships was controversial – the crowd booed their marks when they were placed ahead of two Canadian teams – the German's technique and finesse also worked to win them that medal. The 1984 Russian Olympic pair champion Oleg Vasiliev hinted that they probably should have retired after the Vancouver Olympics, because he feels there is a different type of pair skating now that is more powerful and artistic and "more extra." Still he respects their abilities in spite of uncertain training conditions. "They skate fast, very quiet," he said. "You can't really hear any scratch on ice. They did triple-triple [jump] sequence, they do difficult lifts, even the twist is better right now, but not comparable to Volosozhar and Trankov and the Canadians."

Teamed up in May of 2003, Savchenko and Szolkowy were an odd combination of past lives and skills. She was born in the Ukraine, the daughter of a former weightlifter, and the only athlete among four children. A determined sort from the beginning, Savchenko had to board a bus at 4 a.m. for a two-hour ride to a rink that was 50 kilometres away to skate. At 13, she started pair skating, attracted to the athletic elements of the sport. She went through the Ukraine system, but was frustrated by lack of support from her country. But she has persisted. "Do not stand in her way when it comes to the goal," her coach Ingo Steuer once told a Russian journalist.

Szolkowy's mother was an East German nurse who met his father, a Tanzanian doctor, when he was a student in the country. When Szolkowy was matched with Savchenko, they had to adjust to each other's styles, but it didn't take them long to become contenders at the highest international levels. They were sixth at the 2005 world championships, then won their first Grand Prix gold medal at Skate Canada during the 2005-2006 season. Savchenko was granted German citizenship on Dec. 29, 2005, making it possible for them to compete at the 2006 Olympics in Turin for Germany. They finished sixth.

But Savchenko and Szolkowy had barrelled their way to the top levels of their sport despite having to overcome more roadblocks than anybody else in the upper echelons: lack of financial support, lack of ice time, lack of peace.

Most athletes are able to bury themselves in their work, while the outside world continues on apace. But for years, Savchenko and Szolkowy have had to deal with the fallout of their coach's distant past as an informer for the Stasi or the German secret police at a time when he was a young athlete training in East Germany, dependent on state support. Steuer's past welled up like a geyser just before the Turin Olympics, when the German Olympic committee feared a loss of reputation from allowing a former Stasi informant to coach German soldiers. At the time, Szolkowy was a member of the German army and his skating was financed by them.

Steuer had to go to court for the right to be with his athletes in Turin and the court ruled in his favour, but he was not allowed to wear the German team uniform. Eventually, Szolkowy had to resign from the Germany army in order to stay with Steuer, and since then, the team has had to raise finances from sponsors and by performing in as many shows as possible. Then they stumbled into an impossible situation during

the 2011-2012 season when Savchenko ruptured a muscle fibre in her left upper thigh, probably attempting throw triple Axels in practice. Yet if they withdrew from the subsequent European championships in Sheffield, England because of injury, would they be able to take part in Art on Ice skating shows, which would pay them money they badly needed to train? They feared the same kind of ban that Evgeny Plushenko was handed by the International Skating Union when he withdrew from the 2010 world championships in Turin, citing injury, but performed in shows after the event, without permission from the Russian federation. With this worry in mind, the Germans went to the European championships but Savchenko aggravated the injury while doing a pair spin in practice and they had to withdraw.

A German court eventually allowed Steuer to don the German uniform when it ruled that he had suffered considerable damage from an inability to train his athletes who had joined the army, while the state was not significantly affected. After all, it said, Steuer held no positions in the army, but acted as an external advisor.

Savchenko and Szolkowy won the 2012 world championship two months later, even after Szolkowy had lost a court case seeking reinstatement to the army – because the court ruled he did not have an authorized coach. Steuer receives no financing because of his Stasi record. (In a recent documentary, "The Diplomat," Steuer said Stasi officials came to his home when he was 17, and pushed papers in front of him to sign to become an informant. Steuer said he saw only the word "prison" in the documents and signed it, acknowledging that if he did not do this, he would not have had the sports career that he did have, winning the 1997 world championships with Mandy Woetzel.) Steuer has suggested to Savchenko and

Szolkowy that they seek help from another choreographer but they steadfastly stick to him, convinced that he is the key to their success.

As if all that wasn't enough to stall a career, Savchenko and Szolkowy have difficulties finding ice time to train in Germany. Their rink in Chemnitz takes out the ice after the world championships for two months and reopens in the summer. In April of 2012, coach and pair team headed to Coral Springs in Florida to work where they choreographed their short program. They spent 2 ½ weeks there in April and another 2 ½ weeks in July and August. The place was half an hour from a beach, a rare treat for the Germans. It was a place where they could relax. Finally.

Tatiana **Volosozhar** & Maxim **Trankov**

Russia

Born: Volosozhar: May 22, 1986; Trankov: Oct. 7, 1983

Coach: Nina Mozer

Best Result: 2013 world champion

THEIR CAREERS WERE TOUGH ENOUGH BEFORE TATIANA VOLOSOZHAR AND MAXIM TRANKOV JOINED FORCES IN MAY OF 2010, IMMEDIATELY BECOMING RUSSIA'S BIG OLYMPIC HOPE IN A FIGURE SKATING DISCIPLINE CLOSE TO THE COSSACK HEART: PAIR SKATING.

THROUGHOUT THEIR CAREERS, THE ARRESTING TEAM FUMBLED, SLIPPED AND fell, met with disaster and buried their heads in their hands. That all changed at the 2013 world championships, when the pair won with the greatest of ease, by 20.15 points. (However, they couldn't get through the program without one slip. Trankov fell after Volosozhar had landed a giant throw triple Salchow, but the miscue cost them little, really. "Tania landed the throw so beautifully that I was rushing to catch up with her and my body went ahead of my legs," he explained. "Apparently we can't do a competition without a deduction this season.") The win didn't make them arrogant or overconfident, however. "We don't think one competition can change everything," Trankov said. "We just won this one. Next year, there will be another competition. The Germans [silver medalists Aliona Savchenko and Robin Szolkowy] are very strong couple….and they know how to fight. Next season, it will be next season. We won, yes, but before, the Germans have four world titles."

Still, the win meant more than a victory to a couple that had finally found its place in the skating universe. For Trankov, it was a strike for artistic, rather than completely athletic skating, the apparent direction of figure skating. "I learn the old school of Russian skating," Trankov said. "And for me, it is most important to get it back. I love to watch the traditional pair skating.

"For me, it is important because I want to take it back to the ice. I want more and more couples to skate traditional pair skating, not like acrobatic pairs."

The very first Russian or Soviet pair to win the Olympic gold medal was Ludmila and Oleg Protopopov in 1964. With their artistic style, they started a dynasty of Olympic and world pair champions. Together, Volosozhar and Trankov promised to carry the torch, to be exquisite, to skate with their souls, but along the way, they have found the path to the Sochi Games more full of potholes than a Ukraine highway. So many times, they have been so close to ultimate success, but just as they seem about to grasp the golden ring, disaster strikes. They have sometimes been the citizens of misadventure.

Example? They were shoo-ins to win the Grand Prix Final, the Olympic test event in Sochi in December of 2012, especially since four-time world champions Savchenko and Szolkowy of Germany were out because of illness. The Russians did win, after all, but in a way they'd rather forget. In the free skate, Trankov's edge slipped on the landing of a triple toe loop jump, and he slid across the ice on his behind. The worst came later, just as he was about to launch Volosozhar into a lofty triple throw Salchow when he fell backward. Fortunately, Volosozhar had hardly been lifted off the ground. She was able to straddle his body and keep her sharp blades away from his face and body. Stunned, the couple fumbled and groped for each other in confusion. It took the pair a long time to regain their composure and get back into the program. When they finished, Trankov buried his face in his black gloves, with a dazed look that comes from having watched your own nightmare and Volosozhar kindly comforted him. He also hurt his leg and hip during the falls. They didn't win this free skate, but had enough points from the short program to win. They won't want to take this memory to the Olympics.

But they have overcome much harder life experiences. Trankov was born in Perm, the son of athletes. His father was a two-time Russian show-jumping champion back in the 1970s and 1980s, his mother a 400-metre hurdler. Perm, the sixth-largest city in Russia in the Ural Mountains, was a good city to start figure skating and his parents wanted him to take up a sport. Although his father taught him to ride a horse, Trankov gravitated to the rink. His father always hovered, trying to teach him about figure skating from his equestrian background.

Trankov had the chance to leave home when he was 15, and he took it, travelling to St. Petersburg. He'd been invited to skate with Irina Ulanova, the daughter of world and Olympic pair champion Alexei Ulanov.

Those early years in St. Petersburg from 1999 to 2001 didn't give Trankov a pampered existence, even though he'd found his way to one of the great pair-producing cities in the world. He was a homeless urchin for three years, sleeping at night in the rink stands and the coaching room. He'd tell his parents that he was living in the dorms. If he'd told them the truth, his mother would have dragged him back home to Perm, he told a reporter. His parents didn`t have the money to move to St. Petersburg with him, he said. His father was an auto mechanic, his mother works with children. It was too difficult logistically.

Trankov didn't mind the hardship. He had his freedom, which was most important to him at the time. He chummed around with Alexander Smirnov (now the partner of Yuka Kavaguti), and admits he hardly trained for the first three years. A friend in St. Petersburg sometimes would help him out with meals and shelter if he needed it. Smirnov's parents would visit and bring jars of home pickles and other tasty treats. Sometimes they survived on leftovers from the kitchen, after having befriended waitresses.

Eventually, Trankov split with Ulanova, after a growth spurt hampered her ability to jump. When told by a former Perm skating acquaintance that he should move to the United States to team up with an American girl, he sought a visa but was turned down. He would have had to wait another six months for a chance to re-apply, but in the meantime, he realized he really didn't want to leave St. Petersburg anyway.

Trankov then hooked up with Maria

Mukhortova, with whom he won the 2005 world junior championship pair title in Kitchener, Ont. Their career seemed destined for success – another Russian pair on the rise perhaps – but he and the slight, blond Mukhortova clashed like oil and water. They didn't gel immediately as a team and they began to wonder if getting together was a silly mistake. Then they struggled with coaching changes. Emotional, perhaps headstrong, they needed a strong coach to put them in their place, and so ended up in the court of famed Olympic coach Tamara Moskvina. But when they started to lag behind Moskvina's schedule, Moskvina became disenchanted after only four or five months, and handed them off to her old star pupil Artur Dmitriev, a two-time OIympic pair champion. "Frankly, if I were her, I would have kicked us out even earlier," said Trankov. Basically, Moskvina had fired them a couple of days after she took on Kavaguti and Smirnov, who she thought had all the right stuff to develop into future champions.

But Dmitriev was busy with television shows and the young team ended up training much of the time on their own. They weren`t experienced enough to pull it off. They considered retirement.

Another esteemed Russian coach, Tatiana Tarasova, urged the team to continue and skate with former Olympic champion Oleg Vasiliev, who had trained 2006 Olympic champions Tatiana Totmianina and Maxim Marinin. With the Russian Olympic champions retired, Vasiliev took on the new team in December, 2006. It worked well, with Vasiliev sending them back to the drawing board, teaching them basic skating skills for the first two months. Trankov admitted he hadn't learned them properly back in Perm. The team won the Russian championships,

finishing almost 14 points ahead of the silver medalists in early 2007.

There was so much promise, but so many wrinkles in Mukhortova and Trankov's star-crossed career. A series of injuries derailed Trankov`s hopes, the worst of which was a dislocation of the first cervical vertebra, the one that holds the head. The injury put the team`s future in doubt, again so much so that Mukhortova tried out with a French skater. When the tryout didn't work out, she returned to skate with Trankov, as if nothing had happened. This irked Trankov.

The team finally made a breakthrough at the 2009 Eric Bompard Grand Prix event in Paris, defeating world champions Aliona Savchenko and Robin Szolkowy of Germany. However, they finished seventh at the Vancouver Olympics. After Trankov fell on a triple toe loop in the short program, he held his head in his hands and skated away from Mukhortova. Only eighth, the chances of a medal had grown quite slim. He knew that although that was his first Olympics, it was also his last with Mukhortova.

After the end of the season, Trankov told a Russian journalist that he felt his opinions hadn`t been considered and he didn`t play a role in any of the decision-making during training. He felt betrayed by his team, although he admitted he was often wrong. He and Mukhortova were equally temperamental, he said, but he was more concerned that Mukhortova wasn't enthused about hard work. Grateful for the seven years that they`d skated together, Trankov knew he had to move on.

Volosozhar didn`t come from a family with golden-lined pockets either. Born in Dnipropetrovsk, the city once regarded as "the closed city" in Ukraine because it had been a carefully guarded militia centre for the Soviet Union, Volosozhar began skating at age four. Teachers were initially dismissive of a girl they thought a tad chubby. Her mother, who also worked with children, took Volosozhar and her sister to public skating sessions for the benefit of their health. Volosozhar's mother was a big fan of figure skating.

Eventually, at age 14, Volosozhar began to skate pairs and trained with her first partner, Petr Kharchenko in Dnipropetrovsk in very poor conditions before they were able to move to Kiev. Volsozhar's mother went with her. Money was in short supply, but Volosozhar didn't know that there was a different way to live. For her, it was normal. Her parents' credo: there were things more important in life than money.

In Kiev, she worked with coach Galina Kukhar, whose assistant was a young skater, Stanislav Morozov. Eventually Volosozhar began to skate with Morozov, but their pairing was romantic, too. In their first season together, they were fifth at the European championships, but by 2007 they had finished fourth at the world championships and were starting to attract attention. They were a striking pair, Morozov with his burly power and strength and Volosozhar with her calm athleticism. Morozov was able to toss the tiny Volosozhar high into the air on triple twists – one of the best in the business. And lifts? Morozov could pick her up and set her down with one hand, as if she was a feather.

But conditions deteriorated in Ukraine so much that they could find only one rink in which to train, and that wasn't easy. "You can't get to the entrance," Morozov told a journalist. "You need to jump over holes. It's like a precipice."

They moved to train in Chemnitz, Germany with Ingo Steuer, once the Ukrainian federation agreed to some of the financing, and then started winning Grand Prix medals. They finished eighth

at the Vancouver Olympics, just behind Mukhortova and Trankov. Morozov, then 31, decided to retire. The pair did not even go on to the world championships, but did a few shows together. However, Volosozhar, still only 23, wanted to skate at one more Olympic Games. "I don't want to skate for Ukraine after [Vancouver] Olympics," Volosozhar said. There was little money to go around for training and Ukraine did not have a partner that could match her.

"Ukraine now is like Russia in the 1990s," Trankov said. "They have lost everything, good sportsmen." Coaches had left, too. "And if you want to be a good skater, you must pay for programs, because they skated in Germany and must pay Ingo."

Trankov was sure he would stop. But one day he had a private meeting with Morozov who asked him what he wanted to do after Vancouver. "I said: 'I will stop,'" Trankov told him.

Morozov said: "If I invited you for Tatiana, you will continue your sport?"

"For sure I would continue," said Trankov, who had asked to skate with Volosozhar in 2006. But he was told it was unlikely she would leave her partner/paramour. Later, Trankov asked Morozov if that was true. Morozov told him he would have stepped aside, if it would have meant that Volosozhar could have risen to the top.

In July 2010, the dream team came together. They both gave up what they had known in their previous lives. Volosozhar moved from Germany to Moscow to train with coach Nina Mozer, a highly underrated coach if there ever was one in Russia. Trankov left his beloved St. Petersburg.

Shouldn't it have been easy, finally? It wasn't. They came from different skating schools with different styles. The technique for throws and lifts was different. Morozov was more of a power

lifter than Trankov. When the newbies first tried pair spins, they were a mess. "Only the death spirals were okay," Trankov said. Volosozhar, at 5-foot-3, was a little shorter than Mukhortova, and Trankov at 6-foot-2 was taller than Morozov.

Still, they could not compete internationally anyway. Volosozhar had to wait a year after her last competition for Ukraine (the Vancouver Olympics) to be able to skate for Russia – as long as Ukraine released her. It did. She also received Russian citizenship in Dec. 2010, through an expedited program. Her first language is Russian, and she has Russian ancestry.

Meanwhile, they got in some valuable

experience in small competitions in Russia, then made a bold statement when they won the Russian championships over veterans Yuko Kavaguti and Alexander Smirnov (two-time world bronze medalists and fourth at the Vancouver Olympics). Still, Volosozhar and Trankov had to miss the entire Grand Prix season, as well as the European championships. On Feb. 16, 2011, Volosozhar finally became eligible to skate for Russia. They had to qualify for the world championships by achieving a minimum score in a recognized international event, and they were able to do that in the Mont Blanc Trophy in Courmayeur, Italy. They won by an astounding 63 points.

Off they headed to the 2011 world championships in Tokyo, three weeks early to become acclimatized to Japan. But a short time after they landed, Japan suffered the earthquake and tsunami that devastated the country in March, 2011. Russia lost contact with its budding stars, but within three days, the lines of communication reopened.

As it turned out, the world championships were moved to Moscow, where, in their first major competition, Volosozhar and Trankov won the silver medal behind Savchenko and Szolkowy. Neither had won a world medal before.

"For us, it was like gold," Volosozhar said.

"We dream about the podium [perhaps winning a bronze], but we finish in second place," Trankov recalled. "It was amazing."

Most impressive was the enthusiasm of spectators, even before their short program, in which they finished third. "I'll never forget how they gave us a standing ovation after the free program," Volosozhar said.

The pair glow when they are together, off and on the ice. "We are happy to be together," Trankov said. "We are happy to skate together every day and see each other on the ice and out. We can go out together somewhere, theatre, movies, some dinner and we never tire about each other."

They are best friends. They talk about everything, they say.

At this point, Trankov does not want to remember the bad moments. Life with his previous partner seems like 10 years ago, he said. "Now I have my new partner and my new life and I don't want to go back to the past." Volosozhar is a calming influence: Trankov impetuous and creative, a poet. He's well read and thoughtful. They live in the same apartment building in Moscow, only a two-minute walk from the rink in which they train in Moscow.

Still, nothing is ever easy for Volosozhar and Trankov. At the 2012 world championships in Nice, France, they both fell on a death spiral, which plunged them into eighth place in the short program. They rebounded with a vengeance, to win the free skate with their riveting Black Swan routine, but took the silver medal again, by only .11 points behind Savchenko and Szolkowy.

They both dealt with injuries in 2011, when they finished second, behind Savchenko and Szolkowy again, missing gold by only .18 points. And Grand Prix Final wasn't their only poor performance. They won Cup of Russia as well, but missed both jumping passes and a throw triple Salchow. Mind you, their program the next year was far more challenging than the last, when they were just starting to feel their feet together.

But they smell gold. They are so close. The Olympic Games in Sochi is the carrot that leads them. With this pair, it won't be a boring trip. And if they win, it will be a reward for everything that came before it.

Ekaterina **Bobrova** & Dmitri **Soloviev**

Russia

Born: Bobrova: Mar. 28, 1990; Soloviev: July 18, 1989

Coach: Alexander Zhulin, Oleg Volkin

Best Results: 2013 European champions, third at 2013 world championships

*I*T SEEMS THAT EKATERINA BOBROVA AND DIMITI SOLOVIEV HAVE BEEN DANCING TOGETHER FOREVER.

BY THE TIME OF THE SOCHI OLYMPICS, THESE RUSSIAN ICE DANCERS WILL BE COMPETING IN THEIR 14TH SEASON TOGETHER. "HE IS MY FIRST AND ONE PARTNER IN FIGURE SKATING LIFE," SAID BOBROVA IN HER DEEP, THROATY VOICE.

Matched together in 2000, they won the 2007 world junior championships in their first appearance. But it took them another six years to win their first medal at a world (senior) championship when they took bronze at the 2013 event in London, Ont. That year, they also won the European championship title for the first time.

They both started out as singles skaters, learning in the same group in Moscow, where they were born.

People in Russia seem to start skating for the same reason: to improve their health. "You know in Russia, we have health group," Bobrova said. Besides, Bobrova's parents were avid sports types: her mother, Natalia, a track athlete on the Soviet team, her father, Alexander, an alpine skier. Her sister, Svetlana, first joined the skating group but little Katya (short for Ekaterina) started to learn to swim at age three. Wistfully, she would watch her sister head off to the rink. When Svetlana came home, Katya would hug her sister's skate boots, clearly in love. Finally, her mother relented, and allowed her to skate, too.

Soloviev began skating with some friends on a lake in a nearby park and then he joined the health group. He was a singles skater until one day, while working in the gym, lifting weights, a metal bar fell onto his head, giving him a concussion. Doctors told him he had to stay off the ice for a month. No longer able to do jumps and spins, Soloviev turned to ice dancing.

About the same time, when she was 10 years old, Bobrova realized singles skating wasn't her forte. Jumps were difficult. She found an ice dancing partner "that was not Dima" – as Soloviev is called. But Bobrova's mother began to call up Dima's mom to ask if he would skate with Katya.

Their partnership began from a meeting of mothers' minds, but at first, Soloviev was very reluctant. At first he said no to the idea of skating with Katya. "I said never will I skate with girls," he recalled. "No. How can I touch her hand? No, no, no, no. It was wrong time." He was 11. When his mother told him that he'd have to go to school and learn to be a teacher, he said he'd try, just this

one time. "I will come and that's it." He actually tried out with a girl other than Katya, and told his mother he liked ice dancing. Somehow the mothers got them together anyway.

The partnership didn't come together easily. In the early years, they fought. They didn't understand each other. "We don't understand that we must work together," Bobrova said. "When we grew up, we understand we can't do this if we are every time fighting."

"If you want to have good placements, we must be strong together, we must help each other," Soloviev said.

With coaches Elena Kustarova and Svetlana Alexeeva, Bobrova and Soloviev floated up the skating ladder, winning Cup of China in 2011, and picking up a pair of seconds in 2012 Grand Prix events. They qualified for two Grand Prix Finals, but languished at the bottom. Only 15th at the Vancouver Olympics, Bobrova and Soloviev rose from eighth at the 2010 world championships to seventh in 2012. But with the Olympics looming in their home country, they knew they needed a turbocharge.

Bobrova and Soloview knew their old coaches were like family to them, after having been with them so long. "They are like second parents," Bobrova said. "But after the 2012 worlds, we know we must change something, because everybody start to talk about Bobrova-Soloviev already die in figure skating."

Soloviev started to think about how they could change so that they could believe in themselves again.

Enter coach Alexander Zhulin, an Olympic silver medalist who had lost Russia's other top dance team, junior world champions Elena Ilinykh and Nikita Katsalapov to Nicolai Morozov at the end of the 2010-11 season. He said in a Russian interview that he lost four kilograms after losing not only them, but French skaters Nathalie Pechalat and Fabian Bourzat at the same time. He said it was a feeling worse than divorce.

At their first practice with Zhulin, "it was like another life in figure skating," Bobrova said. They spent two hours perfecting one step. They found Zhulin's new technique endlessly fascinating. "Two hours went by in one second," Bobrova said. "When I came home, I said: 'Mom, yes, I like it. I believe that we can do this."

Soloviev said that after meeting with Zhulin and determining their new direction and their new style, they had goosebumps. With him, they illustrate a story, something they'd never done before. They did everything he asked, willingly. On the ice, Zhulin illustrated moves that they should do. "He do something with hands, head, whole body and dancing," Soloviev said. "He was so shining, in our eyes."

At Zhulin's school, Bobrova and Soloview work with an extensive team of coaches that includes Zhulin's trusted sidekick, Oleg Volkov, Sergei Pethukov, known as the choreographer for two-time world champions Albena Denkova and Maxim Staviski, of Bulgaria, and Staviski himself. "It's very cool when I wake up and go to practice, I want to go to my practice," Bobrova said. "I know it will be interesting."

Zhulin worked wonders with the team. As talented technically as they were, Bobrova had a habit of slouching, her shoulders forward, her butt sticking out. Zhulin straightened her up, and gave them a new look, down to the costumes and hair styles.

Now with their successes, Soloviev is financially helping out his mother, who worked hard as a translator for him to make money so that

he could skate. His father died when he was one month old. Soloviev has a son, Alexander, from a former marriage.

Bobrova said the bronze medal they won at the 2013 world championships is a confidence booster, and they plan another eye-opener during Olympic season. "We want to try to change again, every time changing, so the free program is not the same as Canadian, American, Italian," she said. "We make something new."

As for Zhulin, he was pleased that the team skated cleanly, and they took a large step forward in their preparation for Sochi. "Victories bring people together and gives them wings to fly," Zhulin told a Russian reporter. He thinks Bobrova and Soloviev are only beginning. They'll probably stay on for another Olympic quadrennial.

Anna **Cappellini** & Luca **Lanotte**

Italy

Born: Cappellini: Feb. 19, 1987; Lanotte: July 30, 1985

Coach: Paola Mezzadri, Igor Shpilband

Best Results: third at the 2013 European championship, fourth at the 2013 world championship

Anna Cappellini and Luca Lanotte are pocket-sized Italians who have steadily (and emotionally) crept up the ice dancing ladder to become a bother to some of the top teams. Known for their charming, playful routines, they stepped outside of their pleasant little bubble last season to play a deadly temptress and a foolish, besotted lover. In other words, they grew up.

Take their starting poses for their free dances, for instance. They went from a joyful, winsome embrace in their "La Strada" routine the previous year to a dangerous stance in their "Carmen" routine last season, with Cappellini coquettishly throwing her sharp skate on Lanotte's shoulder, beyond playful. They zoomed from a G (general audience) rating to PG (parental guidance suggested) in a flash.

Their "Carmen" dance, to the story of a fiery Gypsy who cruelly spurns the love of a soldier in favour of a dalliance with a glamorous toreador – and is then murdered by jealous rage– was their ticket to the big leagues but also their Achilles heel. When the Italians first unleashed their "Carmen" routine in early fall at a competition in Finland, they said they had no idea that "Carmen" was the program also chosen by the 2010 Olympic champions Tessa Virtue and Scott Moir of Canada. Who would want to throw themselves into direct comparison with the world's best? Still, Cappellini and Lanotte bravely kept their "Carmen."

Their coach Igor Shpilband must have known. Before Cappellini and Lanotte arrived on his doorstep, Shpilband had parted ways with Russian-born colleague Marina Zoueva during the summer of 2012, and left to start his own skating club. Virtue and Moir stayed with Zoueva. Cappellini and Lanotte, who had been sixth in the world at the time, wanted to train with both of them in Detroit, but confronted with a choice, they picked Shpilband to raise their technical standard. Shpilband raised more than that.

They came to him with a free dance, "The Legend of 1900," already choreographed by artistic Italian coach, Paola Mezzadri. The film is an Italian drama about an abandoned boy who grew up on a ship and showed a gift for music, but in the end, goes down with the boat when it blows up and sinks. "We worked with that for a few weeks," Shpilband said. He said he tried to see if he could make it work for them, but decided it would not.

Out came Plan B. In his exhaustive music collection, Shpilband said he had a piece of music to – what else? – "Carmen" that he had always wanted to use for a free dance. He had already had it cut. For Cappellini and Lanotte, he had to adjust the cuts to suit them. "I thought they would be the perfect team to do it," he said. "I see them playing the character very well."

In skating, "Carmen" is an old chestnut that has been used by countless skaters, but in ice dancing, they have tended to portray the fiery relationship between Carmen and the toreador.

Russians Tatiana Navka and Roman Kostomarov used this theme to win the 2006 Olympic gold medal. Shpilband wanted to tell a different story: the relationship between Carmen and the unfortunate lover, the loser. He thought Lanotte could play that part well, and Cappellini, he said, was a very striking young woman, vivacious and believable as a temptress. "The dynamic between them could be very interesting," he thought. Shpilband's version of "Carmen" suited this team.

Unfortunately, early in the season, Cappellini

and Lanotte came face to face with Virtue and Moir at Skate Canada in Windsor, Ont. Virtue and Moir had a few bobbles in the short dance, and – shockingly to the world – the Italians went into the free dance only .01 point behind the Canadians. But with one "Carmen" played against the other, the Italian's version, the more traditional of the two, paled in comparison to the dramatic and evocative Canadian performance.

In a post mortem of the dance event, former high-ranking International Skating Union official Sonia Bianchetti – an Italian – wrote that while Virtue and Moir showed passion and emotion, their routine was "just another love story with a sad end, with Carmen's music playing in the background. There is no doubt that the Canadians technically were superior but from the artistic point of view, I must say that for me, Anna and Luca were the best. I found them both breathtaking."

The judges had their own views. Virtue and Moir outscored the Italians by 9.34 points on the free dance alone – and the Canadians had made mistakes. Interestingly enough, Virtue and Moir took great care to ensure that their Carmen did not die, mindful of an International Skating Union edict that dances must be uplifting, not dirge-like and depressing. At the end of Cappellini and Lanotte's version of the routine, Carmen does "die."

Sad end or not, Cappellini and Lanotte made great strides last season. Lanotte fell on opening twizzles in the free skate at the Grand Prix in Paris, but still took a silver medal and qualified for the Grand Prix Final. There, technical issues held them back, as they lost the rhythm of the music in the footwork section, finished nine points behind Virtue and Moir, but moved to fourth place overall. That meant they were ahead of

Russians Ekaterina Bobrova and Dmitri Soloviev, who they had also outfinished at the 2012 world championships. At the 2013 European championships, the Italians won the bronze medal, only about three points behind the top two Russian team (Bobrova and Soloviev included) perhaps lucky that world bronze medalists Nathalie Pechalat and Fabian Bourzat of France had to withdraw because of injury.

But by the world championships, their work with Shpilband had begun to pay off. They showed up with speed, and lots of expression. Their technical mark at the European championships had been slightly higher than both Russian teams. In the short dance at the world championships, the Italians were only fifth in the short dance behind the ailing French team. But that sizzling "Carmen" routine allowed them to finish third in the free skate, and three points ahead of Bobova and Soloviev in the technical aspect. They finished fourth overall, now bona fide Olympic contenders. Overall, they missed the bronze medal by only 1.15 points.

Shpilband said he did not expect the third-place finish in the free dance, although the goal was to move up in the standings from the time they started to work together during the summer of 2012. "I think they have a new approach in choreography and skating and technique and they try to adapt and learn," Shpilband said. "It makes them stronger skaters. They exceeded all expectations that we had. They are very hard-working kids. "

They are anxious to learn and they pick up every Shpilband word. Although the top two teams in the world are in another class, the fight for the Sochi bronze medal will be desperate among five or six teams. And now Cappellini and Lanotte have put themselves in the mix.

Madison **Chock** & Evan **Bates**
United States

Born: Chock: July 2, 1992; Bates: Feb. 23, 1989

Coach: Igor Shpilband

Best Result: third at the 2013 Four Continents championship, won the 2013 World Team Trophy

MADISON CHOCK AND EVAN BATES ALWAYS SEEM TO SURPRISE PEOPLE. THEY DID SO WHEN THEY JOINED FORCES IN THE SUMMER OF 2011, BOTH WORLD JUNIOR ICE DANCING CHAMPIONS WITH DIFFERENT PARTNERS. SHE WAS A SKATER WITH AN EXOTIC GLOW AND HAWAIIAN BLOOD, HE A LANKY LAD FROM MICHIGAN, coming off an extremely serious injury, a completely severed Achilles tendon that stalled his career, just as things were getting interesting.

It took Bates nine months to get back onto the ice after the accident, in which previous partner Emily Samuelson slid down his back during a practice lift – and her blade ripped down the back of Bates' boot and into his tendon. Bates' recovery was excruciatingly painful: He had surgery, he had to keep weight off the foot for six weeks, he did aquatics. And finally when he did step back onto the ice, it was only for five minutes the first time – this four months after the accident. Samuelson and Bates tried to pick up where they had left off when he did start to train seriously again, but the magic was gone and they split up.

Chock became available when her world junior champion partner, Greg Zuerlein, retired to attend college. Bates was one of a string of males lining up to try out with her. Chock chose Bates, who stands 10 inches taller than her, unusual for an ice dancing team. But somehow it works, and when they finally began to roll in their second season together, they delivered some more surprises: They won the silver medal at the U.S. championships ahead of former world bronze medalists Maia and Alex Shibutani; They finished seventh at the 2013 world championships – although they were sixth in the free dance ahead of former world bronze medalists Nathalie Pechalat and Fabian Bourzat (who arrived with little training from an injury); And they defeated Kaitlyn Weaver and Andrew Poje of Canada to win the dance event at the World Team Trophy in Japan in April.

"It was an unbelievable year," said their coach Igor Shpilband. "It exceeded all our expectations this year, from not being able to make the world [championship] team the year before."

Chock and Bates' first year together was a time to get to learn about each other. They had different styles. Shpilband said they had to blend their skills – and Bates had to take time to work himself back into shape after being away from training for so long. In their second season together, last year, Shpilband had a better idea of

what they could do. "Those two have tremendous potential," said the Russian-born coach. "I believe this is only the first step for them. There is no skater in the world like him."

In an era that includes Tessa Virtue and Scott Moir and Meryl Davis and Charlie White? These top two teams are emblematic of the future of ice dancing: They have small bodies that can turn on a dime to do all of those flying twizzles (travelling rotations) and footwork sequences and transitions. Yes, Bates is tall at 6-foot-2, but Shpilband says that for all of Bates' height, he is quick on his feet and can dance as well as skate. He knows how to use his body, the coach said. And choreographically? There is lots of room for a designer to take advantage of Bates' long legs, skating skills, and deep edges, Shpilband said. "The sky is the limit for him," he said.

As for Chock, she's expressive with beautiful movement. For the Olympic season, they will skate to "Les Miserables" for their free dance.

The music complements them, Shpilband decided. "With Evan being that tall, I'd like to take advantage of his amplitude and power," the coach said. "If he can take full advantage of this, it will be hard for others to match."

The Sochi Olympics, however, is not their ultimate goal: They have their eye on the next Olympics in PyeongChang, South Korea in 2018. Shpilband said he'd rather take the time to develop their skills properly than try to rush them and hide weaknesses with choreography for the short-term. "They have to build a foundation and work toward the next four years," he said.

But the young team – she was 20 at the 2013 world championships, he 24 – can't wipe the smiles off their faces. "I am really proud of Madison," Bates said at the 2013 world championships. "We had more speed, more power. We felt really comfortable. We are looking beyond Sochi." But in the meantime, Chock and Bates will make their presence felt.

Meryl **Davis** & Charlie **White**

United States

Born: Davis: Jan. 1, 1987; White: Oct. 24, 1987

Coach: Marina Zoueva, Oleg Epstein

Best Results: two-time world champions, 2010 Olympic silver medalists

ERYL DAVIS AND CHARLIE WHITE HAVE NEVER DANCED WITH ANYONE ELSE.

HOW COULD THEY? THEY GREW UP IN THE SAME SUBURB, BLOOMFIELD HILLS, MICH., 10 MINUTES APART. THEIR PARENTS ARE FRIENDS. THEY BOTH STARTED AT THE DETROIT SKATING CLUB,

and coach Seth Chafetz paired them up as ice dancers when Davis was a tiny but precocious 9-year-old skater, and White, an 8-year-old hockey-playing boy who just want to enhance his skating abilities. White came to the team with an unusual combination of abilities. He played violin (for himself) and AAA hockey for the Honeybaked Hockey Club, a prominent local organization that had produced a few NHL players. While ice dancing is a rather gentle pursuit, hockey is not. In 2006, White broke his ankle playing hockey, just after he and Davis had won a bronze medal at the world junior figure skating championships and were on the ascent. The ankle injury put a temporary halt to his figure skating career, but one form of skating helped the other. White credits his career playing hockey with an ability to skate very fast. To this day, Davis and White are known for their blinding speed across the ice, and their blurring twizzles.

By the time Davis and White get to the Olympics in Sochi, they will have been together 17 years, like archrivals Tessa Virtue and Scott Moir.

Is it any wonder that the two teams have separated themselves from the rest of the pack?

Davis and White won an Olympic silver medal (in 2010 in Vancouver) before they won a medal of any colour at the world championships, with the help of their "Phantom of the Opera" free skate as well as their very memorable Bollywood short program routine. That East Indian number made more of an impact than any they had ever done. It created a stampede of East Asian non-skating fans to race to YouTube for a look. It tied in nicely with Davis' scholarly interests: she's an anthropology major at university, despite having had to contend with dyslexia as a youngster. She struggled with reading until the 11th grade and she also has problems with depth perception. According to a USA Today report, Davis sticks close to the boards during warmups and practices, not knowing exactly how far away other skaters are. White protects her.

White has his own game. He studies political science and deals with asthma, requiring him to use an inhaler every morning and night and to

declare his prescribed medications to officials.

Currently, Davis and White hold all of the world record scores for ice dancing: short program (77.12, with Virtue and Moir two points behind them); free dance (112.68, with Virtue and Moir only .35 points behind them) and total score (189.56, a healthy 4.52 points ahead of their Canadian rivals). In any other generation, Davis and White would be runaway stars, but over the past few years, the Canadians have won two world titles, the Americans also two. In the game of one-upmanship, the Canadians are on top, with an Olympic victory in 2010. Still, Davis and White have certain bragging rights, steaming along to remain undefeated during the 2010-2011 season, when Virtue and Moir competed at only 1 ½ competitions. (With surgery to repair Virtue's chronic exertional compartment syndrome after the Olympics, the Canadians completed only one competition the following season – the 2011 world championships in which Davis and White defeated them. Virtue and Moir had defeated the Americans in the short dance at Four Continents, but 30 seconds in the free dance, Virtue suffered a tightening of the quad muscle unrelated to her previous problems, and had to withdraw.)

With Virtue and Moir healthy during the 2012-2013 season, Davis and White still remained undefeated, meeting their counterparts three times, and conquering them in the Grand Prix Final (an event Virtue and Moir have never won), the Four Continents championships and the 2013 world championships in London, Ont., in the Olympic champions' own back yard. Davis and White, with their customary brilliance, left no detail wanting.

The two teams are training mates, eying each other every day in Detroit, and friends, so they say. "It's a special rivalry," White said. "Without them, I definitely wouldn't be at the point that I am at. It has pushed us and I like to think in return we've pushed them back."

While on a bus with Moir on the way to a rink years ago, White told Moir the story of his experience playing in a hockey tournament in Canada. A huge brawl ensued. Both benches cleared. Parents were fighting in the stands. White was the only one left sitting on the bench. As he told his Canadian rival the story, Moir said: "You know what? I think I was actually in the middle of that fight on the other team." They both laughed. Moir remembers the American skaters from a novice-level competition at Lake Placid, N.Y. a dozen years ago. "It's been quite a ride," Moir said. "But I agree with Charlie. We use each other every day in practice. It's nice to be able to talk to each other in the change room and know exactly what we're going through. It's really hard to slack off when you have these guys out there, going 100 miles an hour around the ice."

They are so similar in many respects, so different in others. Russian-born Marina Zoueva oversees both of them, managing the duelling factions that are sometimes on the ice together, sometimes not. "They are so different in their character, their temperament, their physical and artistic abilities," Zoueva said. "I love them both. When I'm watching Charlie and Meryl, they touch my soul. When I'm watching Tessa and Scott, I forget about the stopwatch [to time lifts]. I just melt away."

Elena **Ilinykh** & Nikita **Katsalapov**
Russia

Born: Ilinykh: Apr. 25, 1994; Katsalapov: July 10, 1991

Coaches: Nikolai Morozov, Denis Samokhin

Best Results: second at the 2013 European championships, 2010 world junior champions

ELENA ILINYKH AND NIKITA KATSALAPOV HAVE ALL THE RIGHT TOOLS TO BE THE NEXT STARS OF RUSSIAN ICE DANCE, BUT FOR SOME REASON, THEY HAVE BEEN LOSING THEIR WAY. ONCE THOUGHT TO BE RUSSIA'S BEST HOPES IN ICE DANCING FOR THE SOCHI GAMES, THIS EXQUISITE TEAM BOMBED AT THE 2013 WORLD CHAMPIONSHIPS, FINISHING NINTH. A COUPLE OF MONTHS EARLIER,

they had won the free dance at the European championships enroute to the silver medal. That day in Zagreb, Croatia, they defeated Ekaterina Bobrova and Dmitri Soloviev, who went on to take the bronze medal at the 2013 world championships.

Could have. Should have. But they haven't.

In the musical chairs of coach trading that occasionally happens everywhere, Bobrova and Soloviev had ironically switched to former world champion Alexander Zhulin, the coach that Ilinykh and Katsalapov had left in a huff in May, 2011, unhappy that their programs weren't ready for the following year, that they hadn't been getting enough attention, according to Russian reports. Zhulin had been busy, involved with skating shows, as well.

The history of Ilinykh and Katsalapov has been one of interruptions, precocious moments, programs that perhaps didn't work for them, or that they didn't execute, and deep disappointments. Yet here they are, an attractive couple with a soft glide over the ice and those nice airy knee flexions that are vital to an ice dancer. And they're artistic. And they've worked with some of the best.

Katsalapov had started as a singles skater in Moscow, but couldn't handle triple Lutzes and triple flips. Ilinykh had been a singles skater, too, but her coach at the time thought dance offered a better future for her. She was originally partnered with Ivan Bukin, a dead ringer for his father, Andrei Bukin, who won the 1988 Olympic gold medal in ice dancing with the fiery Natalia Bestemianova.

Fate took a different road, however, when 2002 world champions Irina Lobacheva and Ilia Averbukh matched Katsalapov up with Ilinykh when they were barely teenagers, and became their first coaches. And herein lies the tale of their life: In 2005 they went to a training camp run by Zhulin at the time he was preparing Tatiana Navka and Roman Kostomarov for the Turin Olympic season. The youngsters were inspired by the experience, but juvenile squabbles between the two split them up. Katsalapov

skated with another partner, while Ilinykh headed to the United States and worked with a less talented Russian skater for a couple of years under Marina Zoueva and Igor Shpilband. When Ilinykh returned to Russia in the spring of 2008, Katsalapov had just broken up with his partner, so they teamed up again, having learned a lesson: that they need to communicate with each other and find compromises. But they had lost two years of togetherness, the factor that is an ace for the discipline's top two teams, Meryl Davis and Charlie White and Tessa Virute and Scott Moir. Ilinykh realized she could not skate without the talented Katsalapov.

Under Zhulin, they were explosive together on their first season on the Junior Grand Prix circuit, winning both of their events and taking silver at the Junior Grand Prix Final. They were on a roll: They won the world junior championship the first time they entered it.

During the 2010-2011 season, Zhulin wanted them to skate a free dance to a classical ballet-themed "Don Quixote." Ilinykh wore a tutu designed by the Bolshoi Ballet. But even more importantly, the team began to work with a Russian ballet legend, Ludmila Vlasova, who now serves as a choreographer for the team.

Vlasova has a life that is the stuff of movies. A soloist in the Bolshoi Ballet during the 1970s, she was married to Alexander Godunov, one of the most brilliant of Soviet ballet dancers. His best friend and former ballet-school mate was Mikhail Baryshnikov, who defected to Canada in 1974. Godunov had already been tagged as a potential defector at about the same time and was not allowed to tour outside the country for years, but in 1979, when the Bolshoi Ballet performed in New York, Godunov slipped away and asked for political asylum. The move created

an international incident. When the KGB found Godunov missing, eight of its steely jawed officials put Vlasova on a plane to Moscow, but the U.S. State Department halted the flight to determine if Vlasova was leaving of her own free will. A flurry of calls went back and forth between U.S. president Jimmy Carter and Soviet leader Leonid Brezhnev, but – after the plane had sat on the tarmac at Kennedy Airport for three days – they all were satisfied that Vlasova wanted to return. The remainder of the Soviet ballet group continued to Chicago on its tour without Vlasova. The Soviet news agency Tass reported that Vlasova had "displayed a feeling of lofty civic duty and courage in the face of police threats and blackmail" on returning. Tass didn't mention the defection of Godunov. Years later, in an interview with a Russian reporter, Vlasova said she could not leave her mother and brother, who had given up their personal lives for her. Godunov tried for a year to get Vlasova into the United States – they had never been apart in the eight years they were together – but at the time, it was impossible. They divorced three years later. Godunov danced in the United States but also acted in a handful of movies, most notably as an Amish farmer in the film "Witness," starring Harrison Ford – and reviewers found him riveting. In 1995, Godunov was found dead in his California home at age 45, of "acute alcohol syndrome."

During the summer of 2012, Russian-born coach Igor Shpilband finally met Vlasova when she spent two weeks in Detroit, where he works. Shpilband, too, had defected to the United States. He was part of Jayne Torvill and Christopher Dean's tour through the United States in 1990 when one of the Soviet skaters, Gorsha Sur, decided to defect. Shpilband and a couple of others decided to join him. When Shpilband told Vlasova about his past, she countered by telling him about her experience with defection. They talked over it until late into the evening one night. "It gave me goosebumps," Shpilband said. "To me, it was more traumatic than Romeo and Juliet."

Vlasova entered the world of figure skating choreography when she got a call from Russian coach Natalia Linichuk, who works in the United States. Vlasova knew nothing about figure skating, but she was hooked when she saw Anjelika Krylova win a world bronze medal with her first partner, Vladimir Fedorov in 1993. Since then, Vlasova has worked with world champions Oksana Grishuk and Evgeny Platov, Marina Anissina and Gwendal Peizerat and Lobacheva and Averbukh.

So there were Ilinykh and Katsalapov soaking up the smarts from one of Russia's most respected ballerinas and choreographers. New coach Nikolai Morozov reasoned that after their short dance at the 2013 world championship, when Katsalapov barely held together his first set of twizzles, that they skated as if air had gone out of the balloon. Their free dance wasn't done with the same energy as they had done it for the European championships and Katsalapov slipped out of a spin. Katsalapov said he had no idea what happened because he said he had trained very well. He said he just couldn't feel the connection with his partner.

With the pressure on and a home Olympics looming, Russian skating federation director-general Valentin Piseev was clearly disappointed in Ilinykh and Katsalapov. They are a very interesting, talented team, he told reporters, but "You need also to work hard. It is something they lack, in my opinion. And not only in mine. You need to work, not only depending on what mood you are."

He said he was sure that if the team changed its preparation system, they would achieve good results. "So far they lack work discipline," he said. Truth be told, working with Morozov comes with disadvantages: He has so many skaters, that he's away from home at competitions with them for weeks at a time. At times, Ilinykh and Katsalapov were training with other coaches. They defended Morozov.

In another interview, Morozov denied Piseev's accusations, and so did Katsalapov, saying perhaps he had given too much in training and had nothing left in the tank for competition day. However, Vlasova had her own take on the situation. Vlasova knew that Zhulin was a workaholic and expected the same from his students. Ilinykh and Katsalapov had to learn that talent is worth only 10 per cent, she said. "The rest is work."

Nathalie **Pechalat** &
Fabian **Bourzat**
France

Born: Pechalat: Dec. 22, 1983; Bourzat: Dec. 19, 1980

Coach: Igor Shpilband

Best Results: two-time European champions, third at the 2012 world championships

FRENCH ICE DANCERS NATHALIE PECHALAT AND FABIAN BOURZAT DARE TO BE DIFFERENT. THEY ARE COURAGEOUSLY DIFFERENT.

THEY COME BLASTING OUT OF THE BLOCKS, LOOKING LIKE MUMMIES, LIKE TIME PIECES, LIKE POLKA DANCERS MARRYING THEIR RHYTHMS TO CAN CAN DANCES, LIKE ROLLING STONES, LIKE DOLLY PARTON/KENNY ROGERS

spinoffs, (fringed chaps included), like circus acts, or like George of the Jungle (okay, that was an exhibition routine, where you're allowed to go over the edge). Pechalat and Bourzat always flirt with the edge. It's who they are.

"I hate classical music. It's boring," Bourzat once said, a man who used to collect beer coasters.

Never mind. They've had very long careers and the time to explore all manner of leitmotifs, life lessons and hardships. When they hit Sochi, they'll be the greybeards of the ice dancing world, with Pechalat being a wise (hopefully) 30 years old and Bourzat, a worldly 33, given that he was born the year of the 1980 Lake Placid Olympics. His life will span 10 Winter Olympics. Not everybody in figure skating can say that.

The trouble is, Pechalat and Bourzat's careers started in another era in figure skating, the world of the 6.0 scoring system. All skaters born in that system had to relearn what was important and required when the International Skating Union ushered in a new system, back in the mid-2000s.

They valiantly rallied and presented routines admirable in their time. But a new young generation growing up with code of points and the necessity of doing athletic, even acrobatic high-flying lifts and whirling twizzles in very which direction, and spins, too, learned the tricks from childhood. Even ice dancers who are now coaches know that their very young students are doing things they never could.

Pechalat and Bourzat are one of the few dance teams remaining from the old school that didn't learn the ambitious elements from the ground up. Incredibly, they've coped, winning a bronze medal at the 2012 world championships in Nice, France, behind two North American teams – Tessa Virtue and Scott Moir and Meryl Davis and Charlie White, who pushed the new wave to its height.

And even more incredibly, Pechalat and Bourzat crept ever closer to the top two at this event, finishing only .85 points behind Davis and White in the short dance. Although the gap widened to 3.59 points after the free dance, still, Pechalat and

Bourzat breathed down the necks of the Americans in the technical mark, behind only a point or so, mainly because of the high degree of execution on their difficult lifts.

"It's hard for them, but I really have a big respect for them to be able to be competitive and to always have great elements," said choreographer/coach Pasquale Camerlengo. He has worked with them, along with his wife, Anjelika Krylova, since the French team felt the need to escape Russia with the stern suggestion from on high that Russian coaches should stick to working with Russian athletes in the leadup to the Sochi Olympic Games. Pechalat and Bourzat picked the Krylova school in Detroit, knowing that the former Russian world champion and Olympic silver medalist was a product of the same school of skating as their previous coach, Alexander Zhulin, making the change less traumatic. (During the summer of 2013, Pechalat and Bourzat moved to coach Igor Shpilband on the direction of French federation president Didier Gailhaguet, but even if the move wasn't their idea, they say they are pleased with the switch nevertheless and feel they have made great progress.)

Besides, although Pechalat had a non-skating friend in Russia with whom she could tour museums or chat over coffee (she studied economics and finance at a prestigious finance university in Moscow), Bourzat felt isolated in a country where he did not speak the language. "If I'm happy on the ice, I'm happy off the ice," he said. "You know why you are there. But sometimes when practice is hard, there is no one to talk to."

To stay competitive with their younger peers, Pechalat and Bourzat have had to work that much harder, raising their technique to be able to do the required elements, and teaching their

bodies to be able to do it well without thinking. They lack the muscle memory of the youngsters. "They were able to adapt themselves," Camerlengo said. "We always have to pay attention. It's hard work to build the programs, to put down things in a smart way."

But the hard work and the strain have taken a toll. In January, Bourzat suffered a partial tear of the adductor muscle of his right leg, causing the team to withdraw from the European championships, which they had won in the two previous seasons.

They stopped training for a month, and when he returned, Bourzat couldn't skate more than 30 minutes a session. Camerlengo said he would have pulled them out of the 2013 world championships as well as the Europeans, because "it didn't make sense for them to go in this kind of condition," but they went to qualify Olympic spots for Sochi. They drew on their experience to finish fourth in the short dance, less than a point out of third. But unable to hold it together for the long free dance, they finished only seventh in the free skate and sixth overall, with Bourzat fumbling with a twizzle, the lifts and spins. They had rocked the practices, when they did it in sections.

"He was in pain," Camerlengo said. "It was clear they were not ready to do it at worlds, but we had to go through it."

Before they even competed at the 2013 world championships, they were looking forward to the Olympics, with ideas for their programs already assembled by February, using their time wisely while Bourzat was addressing his injury. And that's the way this French team tends to do things. Every year, they come to work with Camerlengo and Krylova with ideas; the coaches and choreographers approve them, dismiss them if they think they won't work. "They want to always keep this original style," Camerlengo said. "They want to be unique. They don't want to be compared to others."

And you can be sure, Carmen will be the last music choice they would ever make, Camerlengo said, smiling, referring to the duelling Carmens of two leading dance teams last season. This Olympic season, it's Bob Fosse and music from "Cabaret." Their free dance is the story of "The Little Prince," the most read and translated book in the French language, and also the best-selling book in

the world. It's a wistful tale of a prince in search of knowledge, who finds love, but also thistles. The French ice dancers say the story reflects their skating careers.

Tessa **Virtue** & Scott **Moir**

Canada

Born: Virtue: May 17, 1989; Moir: Sept. 2, 1987

Coaches: Marina Zoueva, Johnny Johns

Best Results: won the 2010 Olympics, two-time world champions

'S WONDERFUL, SO THE SONG SAYS. THAT'S WHAT THEY ARE.

TESSA VIRTUE AND SCOTT MOIR FIRST HELD HANDS WHEN SHE WAS SEVEN AND HE WAS NINE, AND THERE WAS AN INSTANT RAPPORT, EVEN THOUGH THEY RARELY SPOKE TO EACH OTHER FOR THE FIRST WHILE. BY THE TIME THEY COMPETE AT THE SOCHI OLYMPICS, THEY WILL HAVE BEEN

reaching spontaneously for each other's hands for 17 years. And they'll be lauded as the bellwethers of the ice dancing world, painting vivid pictures of what can be done despite the restrictive, exacting rules in ice dancing.

They were the first ice dancers to earn a perfect mark of 10 for program component (presentation) marks in the code of points judging system adopted after the scandals of the Salt Lake City Olympics. They got their 10 at a time when it meant perfection. Several years ago, a slight difference in the wording of International Skating Union rules deemed that a mark of 10 signified an "outstanding" effort. But not perfection. In the words of one international judge, the magistrates of marks now give out 10s "like so much candy. "

Two teams were raking in 10s like marbles on a school sidewalk at the 2013 world championships: archrivals Meryl Davis and Charlie White of the United States and Virtue and Moir of Canada. Between the two of them, they got 33 marks of 10. The rest of the competitors were

buffeted in the wake of their magnificence. Obviously, the polkameisters of the sport still need to be pretty good to get those 10s.

When Virtue and Moir became the first North Americans and the youngest ice dancers (she 20, he, 22) to win an Olympic gold medal at the 2010 Vancouver Olympics, they stopped the hearts of some of the best. "I am proud of ice dancing tonight," said Gwendal Peizerat, who won ice dancing gold at the scandal-plagued Salt Lake City Games in 2002. "It was probably one of the greatest ice dancing competitions I've ever seen." The 1980 Olympic men's champion, Robin Cousins, working for the British Broadcasting Corporation, compared them to 1984 Olympic champions Jayne Torvill and Christopher Dean, who pushed the boundaries of ice dancing with their memorable, creative routines.

"They skate as one," said Ann Shaw, a Canadian who helped set up the code of points for ice dancing and who admitted to goosebumps when she watched their lyrical Gustav Mahler "Symphony No. 5" in Vancouver – not an easy piece to

interpret. "Every movement from one position to another is like the unfolding of a rose," Shaw said. "He just unfolds her to the next position. Every link is smooth and intelligent."

Having reached such heights in Vancouver, Virtue and Moir had a choice: to leave it there and retire, or to continue and try something new each time. Eventually, they felt they had more to give. Sure, they'd like to win again, but their motivation lies elsewhere. They do it for themselves, to see where they can go. They continue to push their craft, just like Torvill and Dean. They set standards. They take risks. They vow never to do the same lift from season to season, remarkably creative, despite the fact that they weren't the right build to do difficult lifts – they are almost the same size. A height disparity would make it easier.

Since the Olympics, their dance roster has been an exercise in variety. The season after the Olympics, their free dance placed together two pieces of music that shouldn't have gone together: a Latin feel "Hip Hip Chin Chin" juxtaposed with Diana Krall's "Temptation." Both were sensual in different ways. They bridged the change in tempo with a riveting combination spin. Next up? "Funny Face," with a Broadway, upbeat, pantomime, dancey feel, an homage to Virtue's childhood idol, Audrey Hepburn. Moir slicked down his cropped hair and didn't just skate like Fred Astaire. He became Fred Astaire, even though as he once said: "I wasn't raised a dancer. I was raised a hockey player."

Then came "Carmen," a risk if there ever was one. Hadn't everyone under the sun in skating resorted to that old saw from the beginning of time? Virtue and Moir boldly made it their free dance and proceeded to unleash a Carmen that nobody would forget: passionate, sizzling,

powerful, sensual to the point of being carnal.

Although their short dance seemed to fly in the shadows of "Carmen, "it too, was no less spectacular, especially by the end of the season, after they had tinkered with it. "And the Waltz Goes On," was a piece composed by acclaimed movie actor Anthony Hopkins. Its haunting sound, deep and rich and emotional, touched them.

Even with all of this good material in hand, Virtue and Moir had a troubled season from beginning to end. Moir injured his neck doing a short dance lift two days before an early season competition in Finland and an hour before the flight was to leave, withdrew, concerned that the trip would worsen the injury. That lift, their final move in the short dance, came back to haunt them at Skate Canada, when the transitions into it didn't go as planned and Moir got a face full of skirt. "Sometimes that lift gets stuck," Moir said. Generally, they left a lot of points on the table. They won the short dance by only one-hundredth of a point over Italians Anna Cappellini and Luca Lanotte, but then went on to win the free dance and the gold medal easily.

They got a one-point penalty for a lift that went too long at Cup of Russia and then they lost the Grand Prix Final. Throughout the season, they continued to alter their routines, refining them, changing lifts, changing all of their footwork sections. At the Canadian championships, they received another two penalty points for two lifts that went too long. Already people had begun to ask if they had lost faith in their programs.

Moir said the risks they took in presenting such difficult programs were worth it. "We wouldn't be skating if we were just going to be playing it safe and doing the same tricks every year," he said.

Still, at the 2013 world championships, they lost again to Davis and White, putting themselves in a hole during the short program when Virtue's twizzles went awry. And they lost marks during their midline step sequence. Their scores all season hadn't matched those of Davis and White and the Americans defeated them for the gold by 4.52 points – in their own backyard.

So was "Carmen" a bad idea? "It was made to be a very difficult program," Moir said. "It was made to be both different for the year and different for us to skate to. Marina really wanted to push us. She didn't want a single move that was easy for us. She wanted us to work."

Moir admitted even some members of their team didn't like "Carmen." The chips didn't fall their way at the world championships. Moir doesn't blame "Carmen."

But "Carmen" was really only a means to an end. "We needed to go there, before we could come here," Virtue said, speaking of their Olympic routines this year. ""We have to be proud that we pushed ourselves and went in a different direction."

And where has "Carmen" led them? This year, Virtue and Moir are back to exquisite classics, doing them as only they can. Coach/choreographer Marina Zoueva had it in her mind for a long time for the Canadian team to skate to the romantics of early 20th century Russian composer Alexander Glazunov, and for a bit of dramatics at the end, contemporary Alexander Scriabin, with a proud piano concerto. The music is her thanks to Russia, where she was born. And Virtue and Moir are the perfect team to carry off the movement, a dramatic contrast to "Carmen" which featured conflict and tattered relationships. This Russian music is all about harmony and coming together and the movement reflects

it. For Virtue and Moir, it is the story of their partnership with all of its ups and downs. The last section is made to be skated in Sochi: the parade to their finale.

The short dance is another charming, playful masterpiece to several duets by Ella Fitzgerald and Louis Armstrong. Virtue and Moir fell in love with the music immediately. The music had meaning to Zoueva as well. The first CD that she bought when she moved to Canada from Russia in 1991 was a Fitzerald/Armstrong disk. "In Russia at the time, you couldn't get CD of North Americans," she said. "It was really difficult to buy, just to hear, because we had a closed border and you couldn't travel."

And Zoueva loved the sound, the variation of the voices in the music. When Zoueva came to Canada, she felt a personal Renaissance; she soaked up western arts like a sponge. "I do appreciate everything that North American give me to grow as a coach and as a person. I still learn," she said.

Is it any wonder that Virtue and Moir feel that they will be among friends in Sochi? They have a Russian fan group that they've connected with a few times. "It's been amazing to see the support from Russia," Virtue said.

Many Russian eyes appreciate their artistic take on ice dancing. Russian legend Tatiana Tarasova thinks Virtue and Moir will be very strong this season. She doesn't think it fair that they lost the 2013 world title. "I liked them better than Davis and White in the free dance," she told a Russian reporter. "The judges were unable to receive 'Carmen,' as they should have. I think it was an exceptional dance."

Former world ice dancing champ Alexander Zhulin, who coached the third-place team, Ekaterina Bobrova and Dmitri Soloviev, says he gets tired of repeating which team he prefers among the top two: It's Virtue and Moir.

Virtue and Moir have a refinement and a completely different way of presenting dance, Zhulin told a Russian publication after the world championships. "I don't belittle the merits of the American duo, but Davis and White are more of athletes," he said, "And Virtue and Moir are more of artists. I always prefer artists.

"Davis and White are an amazing, brilliant team," Zhulin continued. "They do everything great and with ease, but Virtue and Moir are Virtue and Moir. I simply love them."

'S marvelous, they are.

Kaitlyn **Weaver** & Andrew **Poje**

Canada

Born: Weaver: April 12, 1989; Poje: Feb. 25, 1987

Coaches: Pasquale Camerlengo, Anjelika Krylova, Shae-Lynn Bourne

Best Results: fourth at the 2012 world championships, won the 2010 Four Continents championship

IF YOU HAVE A HEARTBEAT AND A PULSE, IT'S NOT HARD TO SEE WHY KAITLYN WEAVER AND ANDREW POJE GET STANDING OVATIONS ALMOST EVERY TIME THEY DANCE THE NIGHT AWAY.

IT DOESN'T SEEM TO MATTER WHETHER OR NOT THEY ARE IN MEDAL CONTENTION OR THAT THEY LANGUISH IN THE LONG SHADOW OF OLYMPIC CHAMPIONS

Tessa Virtue and Scott Moir, or that they skate despite pestilence and famine. There they are, out on centre ice where they belong, doing what they do, trying to reach hearts.

"On the ice, they give everything," says coach/choreographer Pasquale Camerlengo. "And people see it. It's not enough for them just to perform and do everything. They must give something to the audience."

They started out as wonderkids, matched together and brilliant from the start, she a transplanted American from Houston, Texas, he of Slovak descent (on his mother's side of the family) and the great nephew of Agnesa Burilova. Burilova competed in pairs at the 1964 Olympics before she eventually became coach of Jozef Sabovcik, a Czech who was the 1984 Olympic bronze medalist. Weaver and Poje teamed up in 2006, and started out with a pair of bronze medals on the Junior Grand Prix circuit. Then, competing at the senior level, defied all expectations to win bronze at the 2007 Canadian championships. Despite Weaver dislocating a shoulder

in the warmup before the original dance at the 2007 world junior championships, they earned a bronze medal, and then did double duty, finishing 20th at their first world (senior) championship in 2007.

But the heartbreakers came later, in 2010 when they finished third at the Canadian championships, falling short by only .30 points of getting a spot on the Olympic team for Vancouver. It was especially disappointing because Weaver gained her Canadian citizenship in June of 2009 for that purpose. That placement also took them off the world championship team, too, halting their progress up the international level. They won the Four Continents championships but it was cold comfort. Most of the world's top competitors gave it a miss, coming too close to the Olympic Games. Their dreams had shattered. "To come so close was hard to take," she said.

The following year, with Virtue and Moir on the sidelines, Weaver and Poje lost the national title to Vanessa Crone and Paul Poirier by only 1.03 points. But with their long lines and "Moulin

Rouge" routine, they turned the tables on Crone and Poirier a couple of months later by finishing fifth at the 2011 world championships in Moscow, while their domestic rivals were 10th.

Weaver and Poje were suddenly, finally world and Olympic contenders, no longer after-thoughts. A fourth place finish at the 2012 world championships in Nice, France, the next year, seemed to point toward a podium finish at the 2013 world championships at home in London, Ont., down the highway from where Poje was born.

But then in December, 2012 during practice, Weaver flew into the boards and broke her left fibula. At first, coach Anjelika Krylova thought Weaver's injury was minor, that she'd be back after a weekend's rest. Weaver was whisked off for x-rays, just to be sure. To their shock, the small bone in her leg near the ankle was fractured.

Camerlengo hadn't been there that day; he'd been in France. When Weaver sent him a picture of the x-ray with the fibula, and knowing that she was to have surgery that implanted a plate and a handful of screws on the bone, his first thought was: "Okay, season is over. For me, it was clear, the season is over."

A doctor told Weaver that she need not expect to get her skate boot back on her foot until April, and given that the world championships were in mid-March, he believed it would take a miracle for the team to make it.

"I believe in miracles," Weaver said, and imme-diately set to work, organizing her recovery.

"She want it so bad," Camerlengo said. "The healing process went so fast that she surprised everybody: the physiotherapist, the doctor, she surprised us. She surprised the entire world."

They were forced to sit out the Canadian championships. Weaver appeared, on crutches and a large black cast with a silk flower attached. Poje continued to skate, but motored back and forth from Detroit to Toronto to check on her progress.

Off the ice for two months, Weaver and Poje set out to show up at the world championships, and did. At their first practice, late at night at a secondary rink, with most of their peers giving it a pass, Weaver and Poje practiced. When they took their final bows, the crowd – who had stayed late to watch only them – gave them a standing ovation. Others thought the idea was crazy.

"When we were there, people were saying: 'Why did you bring this thing here? It doesn't make sense,'" Camerlengo said. "[They said] 'They should stay home. There will not be much change for Canada.' But she gave everything she had in that competition. She was in pain. She didn't want to take any drugs to stop the pain. She said she was going to go through with it no matter what."

At first, the goal was just to skate. But before the short dance, Weaver began to talk as if she intended to try to actually compete. Camerlengo said their practices weren't brilliant but the noisy supportive crowds at the Budweiser Gardens puffed them up, gave them a boost. "They were really great," Camerlengo said. "We were so sur-prised by the way they pulled this off."

"We owe so much to the crowd," Weaver said later. "It kept us going. It gave us energy. It calmed our nerves. I can't even believe we are here. We made our dreams a reality."

In the end, Weaver and Poje finished fifth overall, less than two points out of fourth. And they helped earn Canada three spots for dancers at the Olympics. Weaver was still undergoing physiotherapy for the injury at the event – and would be until the plate was removed. The plate and screws also pushed against her foot in the boot.

"It is kind of miracle," Camerlengo said. Each day of her recovery, Weaver had been sending photos of her progress to Camerlengo. They called it "the pic of the day." When she stood on the apron, about to step out for the short dance at the 2013 world championships, Weaver looked at Camerlengo and said: "What about the pic of the day?"

"She was looking around, almost not believing that she is there," Camerlengo said. "She said: 'I am here. What about this picture?'

"I said, 'That's the most difficult picture, absolutely,'" Camerlengo said.

Their season wasn't over. They had always missed the World Team Trophy, but this time they got the assignment in Japan and finished second in the ice dancing portion after Weaver fell on a transitional move. "Just to be able to be here and skate the rest of the season is a gift for us," she said.

Immediately after returning, Weaver headed for surgery on April 16 to have the plate and screws removed from her ankle. For a month after surgery, she was not able to skate. Camerlengo ordered a vacation. This time, their Olympic dream is still alive.

CPSIA information can be obtained
at www.ICGtesting.com
Printed in the USA
LVIC06n1445171213
365739LV00023B/179